CleanWave

A Guide to Success in the Green Recovery

Written by Eric Pasi

No part of this book may be reproduced in any form or by any electronic or mechanical means including information storage and retrieval systems, without permission in writing from the author. The only exception is by a reviewer, who may quote short excerpts in a published review.

The information presented herein represents the views of the author as of the date of publication. This book is presented for informational purposes only. Due to the rate at which conditions change, the author reserves the right to alter and update his opinions at any time. While every attempt has been made to verify the information in this book, the author does not assume any responsibility for errors, inaccuracies, or omissions.

Contents

Preface

Climate Change is the defining crisis of the 21st century. There is no greater threat to humanity, but also no greater opportunity. This issue in particular is very personal to me, and this book reflects my experience but is in no way bound to my story in particular. There are thousands of success stories in clean energy and mine is one among a rising sea of many; and the movement is just getting started.

I was born in Hawaii to two young college students. My dad was an immigrant from Tonga, a small archipelagic nation in the South Pacific, and my mom was a Scandinavian-American from the Midwest. They divorced when I was very young, and I moved back to Minnesota with my mom where we lived with my maternal grandparents, detached from my island roots.

As with many childhoods, mine was pretty complex. I was a multi-racial Polynesian kid in the Midwest, I constantly found myself stuck in the middle. I was different than most everyone else and that was great for the majority of the time, but isolating too. It wasn't until adulthood, after college that I really started to figure out who I am and it's still evolving today.

In 2014, I was fortunate enough to visit my father's former home of Nukualofa, Tonga on the island of Tongatapu. Before the trip, he showed me all the places I needed to see on Google Earth. It was a veritable history of where he and his twelve brothers and sisters grew up; I'd even have the chance to meet an uncle and cousins for the first time; kind of insane. You could tell by the way my dad's eyes lit up how excited he was about it; a big contrast to his usual soft-spoken and humble attitude toward pretty much everything else.

That visit was a whirlwind of emotions. I had just gotten married several months earlier and we were still figuring out our new lives together. My business IPS Solar (more on this later) was at an inflection point where near-term viability was not a foregone conclusion. I was in my father's homeland with no bearings or language skills. All of this contributed to increased anxiety, which I've struggled with off and on most of my adult life.

Tonga is a very beautiful place. But not the Conde-Naste-Travel-Magazine kind of beauty, the beaches aren't perfectly terraformed, you might catch a few sharp rocks between the gaps in your Havaianas. There are no McDonalds. No venti cold presses. No Best Westerns. You won't find vapid cultural appropriation in the name of tourism. There are no Michelin stars. No overly-sanitized, cruise-ready "villages." Just raw beauty at its finest.

On the day of arrival, a few chapters into my beach read we were jolted by a massive 7-magnitude earthquake. It was only a handful of seconds, but it was the first time I'd been anywhere close to an earthquake. This made the whole experience extremely surreal and an immediate reminder of how foreign this place really was. My first thoughts were of the devastating tsunamis that had ravaged Japan and Indonesia. Geographically most of Tongatapu is less than 10-feet above sea level, and I mentally prepared myself to start climbing a palm tree; there was no tsunami.

The next night was very still. The winds were calm and warm. On a midnight walk near our bungalow, I ran into what I thought was some possessed tropical bat. It caused me to spend the next day debating whether or not I needed a pre-emptive rabies shot. Nothing happened of course.

On our last day, my cousin and uncle shepherded us around the island one final time. We stopped at a small clearing just outside the city; it was the ancient ruins of Ha'amonga 'a Maui, one of the country's most sacred landmarks. Like most things in Tonga, the site itself is very modest, with little more than a few signs to identify its significance. The arch-like structure helped to outline the position of sunrise on solstices and equinoxes. This monolith stands in the middle of an island, in the middle of an ocean, a thousand years old, erected as a symbol to my father's people. If you don't know a Tongan person let me tell you that they are proud, strong, happy, and very loving. Despair and fear are not in their vocabulary.

It's near-certain that a more than 2-degree Celsius increase in global temperatures will have devastating impacts globally. It will cause mass migration from warming's most hostile grips, and with it, geopolitical destabilization. It's certain to scorch places like New Delhi, home to tens of millions, where the temperature may regularly climb above 130 degrees. It's certain to swallow many parts of Tonga and other low-lying countries across the world. This is war, it's happening now, and we're losing.

Decades of inaction have hurdled us into our current moment of truth. Can we rise to the challenge or will we fall victim to our own vulnerabilities? Capitalism's "growth-at-all-costs" mantra has afforded the developed world many, many luxuries. But what about our children, and the generations to come?

There are still many barriers today: too much money from entrenched interests, too much misinformation, too much apathy. With America's "Me first." ethos it's difficult to imagine a scenario in which we, as a nation, collectively rise to the occasion and save the world. But the truth is that needed sacrifices will be small and short-lived: retooling industries, retraining workers, shifting the metrics around what a successful economy really means. It's true we have much more to gain from this transition than we do to lose.

The best news you'll hear today is that we have the solutions to solve climate change. For the most part, technology has strained our relationships with each other and the planet over the last few decades. Technology's effect in our daily life cannot be overstated both positively and negatively. But the deployment of clean energy, beneficial electrification, and energy-efficient technology is our opportunity to unlock a future planet that is not only habitable but thriving. In all honesty though, as the author of a book on climate optimism, the science doesn't look good. Some days I doubt we have the grit to do what needs to be done. I don't profess to have all the answers, but we need to have hope.

My dad passed away from heart disease in 2015 at the age of 55, a year after my visit to Tonga. It's something that's affected me in various ways. A few unexpected consequences of his death have been a burst of personal motivation and a lot of perspective. There's a saying that we, everyone on this planet, are all standing on the shoulders of giants, propelled forward into the present by a confluence of our ancestors' struggles and triumphs. How fraught their journeys must have been; facing catastrophes, hunger, and disease. Today we've lost our sense of vulnerability.[1]

The climate crisis threatens not just our future and present, but everything that has ever come before us. We can't let the sacrifices of our fathers, mothers, and their reverence be in vain.

---

[1] Not to mention the devastation imposed on our natural world. Hiding behind screens we're blind to reality outside. Scientists say we're in the sixth mass extinction era, where human-caused climate change, exploitation, and overpopulation have contributed to the loss of more than half of all wildlife since 1970. See Elizabeth Kolbert, *The Sixth Extinction: An Unnatural History* (New York: Henry Holt and Company 2014)

Our ancestors were brave, risking everything to create a better way of life. I like to think we inherited some of that spirit.

Introduction

Thank you, reader, for choosing to pick up this book. Maybe your mom or dad bought CleanWave to help you "find your path," hopefully out of their basement and into a real job. Or, more likely, you're in eighth-grade social studies[2], sometime in the 23rd century learning about the Dale Carnegie of sustainability—me. Regardless of who you are, I appreciate you, and I appreciate your curiosity about joining the clean energy economy.

Because our enemy is silent, invisible, and decades ahead of us, the war against catastrophic climate change *feels* unwinnable. But what normal odds don't account for is the persistent and exponential effort that the clean energy movement is waging.

From 2000 to 2018 US wind and solar capacity increased 4,000% and 55,000% respectively. According to E2's recent Clean Jobs America report,[3] nearly 3.3 million Americans work in clean energy today which is 3 times the fossil fuel industry, and more than the entire populations of Wyoming, Alaska, Vermont, and the Dakotas combined.

---

[2] Shout out Mr. Stevens and Sra. Acosta!
[3] https://www.e2.org/wp-content/uploads/2019/04/E2-2019-Clean-Jobs-America.pdf

The green economy also represents the biggest wealth opportunity of the 21st century, and that's not hyperbole. A *very* conservative estimate from Bloomberg New Energy Finance pegs global spending on clean energy at more than $10 trillion over the next 30 years.[4] That number excludes expenditures on smart grid technology, electric vehicles, energy efficiency, and everything else that constitutes the broad coalition known as "cleantech." Workers in the green economy can expect higher compensation and lower educational barriers for entry.

Now is the time to invest in our people and infrastructure. As we enter a new paradigm, with natural disasters and pandemics fueling global economic volatility, we need the stability and resilience of clean power now more than ever. Recovery efforts already include green energy; from Puerto Rico to the Midwest solar-powered emergency generators and reliable microgrids are powering critical operations. Now is the time to bail out rural America with profitable, diversified income and tax revenues from renewable projects.

More is needed. We must bridge the energy divide between wealthy and under-resourced communities. Under-resourced households pay 2.5 times more for energy as a percentage of their income compared to their wealthier counterparts; modest green improvements could reduce their energy burden by an average of $1,500 annually.[5] From a public health, standpoint reducing emissions could prevent nearly 300,000 premature deaths caused by air pollution *each year*.[6] Most of these preventable casualties occur in historically marginalized neighborhoods

---

[4] https://about.bnef.com/blog/solar-wind-batteries-attract-10-trillion-2050-curbing-emissions-long-term-will-require-technologies/
[5] Kontokosta, Constantine E. and Reina, Vincent and Bonczak, Bartosz, Energy Cost Burdens for Low-Income and Minority Households in Six U.S. Cities: Evidence from Energy Benchmarking and Audit Data (September 1, 2018). Available at SSRN: https://ssrn.com/abstract=3295367 or http://dx.doi.org/10.2139/ssrn.3295367
[6] A truly astronomical number: https://www.nature.com/articles/nclimate2935

where generations of neglect and exploitation have taken their toll. Clean energy has the power to heal.

CleanWave will focus as a guide to those interested in green energy careers in the midst of a post-COVID and racial justice recovery. We'll discuss the current climate and economic crises, the solutions available to address them, and practical advice for prospective job-seekers. Interspersed within the chapters are words of wisdom from industry leaders and myself. At the Afterword's conclusion readers will be armed with the mental ammunition needed for our long fight ahead.

My goal in writing this book, aside from the obvious fame and fortune, is to inspire people because we desperately need talent to win. 24 million new climate-impactful jobs will be created globally by 2030 as a result of addressing the climate crisis.[7] That's more than a few gaps to fill.

CleanWave is also a chance for me to pay forward some of the life-changing opportunities that clean energy has afforded me, for which I'll be forever grateful. This industry is home, and I hope it will be home for you too.

---

[7] https://www.un.org/sustainabledevelopment/blog/2019/04/green-economy-could-create-24-million-new-jobs/

1. The Climate Crisis: A Brief History

"In a chronically leaking boat, energy devoted to changing vessels is more productive than energy devoted to patching leaks."

—Warren Buffett

"If you do not change direction, you may end up where you are heading."

—Lao Tzu

Disco Inferno

As it stands today the future of our planet is bleak. You've heard it on the news: global temperatures are increasing, ice sheets are shrinking, sea levels are rising, the ocean is becoming more acidic. Hurricanes, flooding, drought, fire, and famine have become so common, they're part of everyday life. But when did the climate problem start? How did we get here?

Earth's climate has undergone many changes throughout history. However, according to NASA research, climate variations predating human civilization can all be attributed to natural causes—specifically, very small changes in Earth's orbit, volcanos, and asteroid impact events.

But these observable shifts do not account for our current warming trend. The Earth Science Communications Team at NASA's Jet Propulsion Laboratory reports that "the current warming trend is of particular significance because most of it is extremely likely (greater than 95 percent probability) to be the result of human activity since the mid-20th century and proceeding at a rate that is unprecedented over decades to millennia."

NASA concluded: "The vast majority of actively publishing climate scientists — 97 percent — agree that humans are causing global warming and climate change. Most of the leading science organizations around the world have issued public statements expressing this, including international and U.S. science academies, the United Nations Intergovernmental Panel on Climate Change and a whole host of reputable scientific bodies around the world."[8]

Exactly how are we doing this?

Briefly, scientists attribute the current warming trend observed since the 1950's to the human expansion of the "greenhouse effect," which is when heat radiating from Earth toward space is trapped by the atmosphere, resulting in gradual warming. Certain gases in the atmosphere block heat from escaping—particularly carbon dioxide, methane (gases produced by the production and burning of fossil fuels) and nitrous oxide (produced by fossil fuel combustion, the use of commercial and organic fertilizers, nitric acid production, and biomass burning). In addition, chlorofluorocarbons (CFCs) are synthetic compounds that contribute to the destruction of the ozone layer, and are greenhouse gases.

---

[8] https://climate.nasa.gov/faq/17/do-scientists-agree-on-climate-change/

While CO_2 comprises a tiny part of the atmosphere (nitrogen and oxygen combined make up 99 percent), it's a powerful blocker of radiating energy. Since the Industrial Revolution, humans have increased atmospheric CO_2 concentration by more than a third. This is the most important long-term driver of climate change.

It doesn't take much of an increase in CO_2 to destabilize the planet's fragile ecosystems. According to the National Oceanic and Atmospheric Administration (NOAA), over the past 800,000 years the amount of CO_2 in the atmosphere has fluctuated between about 150 parts per million (ppm) and 250 ppm. The previous record high was about 325,000 years ago, when it hit briefly 300 ppm.

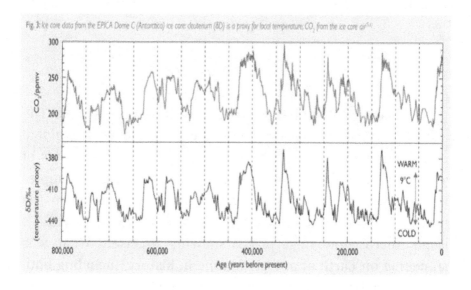

Ice core data from the EPICA Dome C (Antarctica) ice core.[9]

---

[9] https://www.bas.ac.uk/data/our-data/publication/ice-cores-and-climate-change/

Today, both carbon dioxide and temperature levels are higher than at any point in at least the past 800,000 years. Since 1950 CO_2 levels have been increasing precipitously and in 2018 average global atmospheric CO_2 was 407.4 ppm. Correspondingly, the eight hottest years on record

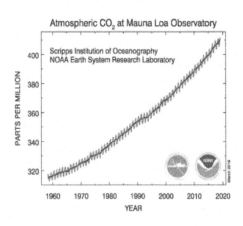

Atmospheric CO_2 at Mauna Loa Observatory

Scripps Institution of Oceanography
NOAA Earth System Research Laboratory

have all happened in the last decade. We're seeing the effects— rising temperatures, rising sea levels, and more violent weather.

Ice, Ice Baby

How can scientists be so sure about these conclusions? The primary method for observing greenhouse gas levels and global temperatures over time, dating back hundreds of thousands of years, is by carefully examining ice. Geologists take core samples from glaciers or ice sheets, which form over time from the incremental buildup of snow. Within these very thin layers are useful microscopic fingerprints showing precisely what was happening on Earth at any given time in history, including both temperature and carbon dioxide (CO_2) levels which have been locked into the ice. We're able to look back hundreds of thousands of years in some areas because these ice sheets are thousands of feet deep.

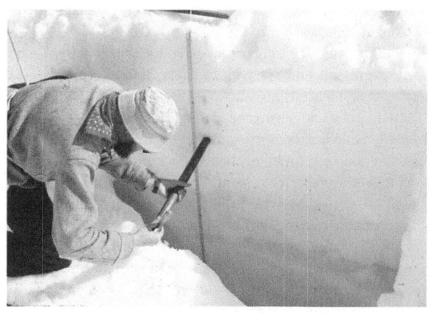

Sampling the surface of Taku Glacier in Alaska.

In the most basic of terms, this means that human intervention is shifting our climate at a rate much more quickly than the world has ever seen before.

Reality Bites

Carbon-based fuel is any fuel that contains the element carbon. As an element, carbon is necessary for life. After hydrogen, helium, and oxygen, it's the fourth most abundant element in the universe by mass. Carbon's unique diversity of organic compounds, and its unusual ability to form polymers, allows it to serve as a common substance of all known life. By mass, it's the second most abundant element in the human body after oxygen.

There are two primary types of carbon-based fuels: biofuels and fossil fuels.

Biofuels are derived from recent-growth organic matter such as corn or grasses, and are typically harvested and processed. Examples of biofuels include ethanol (often made from corn in the United States and sugarcane in Brazil), biodiesel (vegetable oils and liquid animal fats), green diesel (derived from algae and other plant sources), and biogas (methane derived from animal manure and other digested organic material).

Fossil fuels are also organic, but they originated millions of years ago and are extracted from the ground. The principal fossil fuels are oil, coal, and natural gas.

Both types contain carbon. When they're burned—such as in an automobile or a coal-fired power plant—carbon atoms combine with oxygen atoms to form CO_2, a powerful greenhouse gas as discussed earlier in this chapter.

Biofuels are "renewable" in the sense that you can always grow more corn to process into ethanol. But the *combustion* of renewable biofuels produces the same byproducts—including greenhouse gases—as the combustion of fossil fuels.

For people and organizations with ties to the carbon energy industry, progress can be painful. In terms of revenue, the global oil and gas drilling sector is gigantic. Investopedia puts the industry's 2017 worldwide gross domestic product (GDP) at somewhere between $75 trillion and $87.5 trillion.[10] That's stupidity-level money considering 2018 US GDP was roughly $20 trillion. The people who pocket trillions will not go gentle into that good night. It's not simple for the carbon energy complex to admit that times have changed and to move on. Wealthy industrialists and their intermediaries have been fighting against disruption, and they'll continue to do so.

---

[10] https://www.investopedia.com/ask/answers/030915/what-percentage-global-economy-comprised-oil-gas-drilling-sector.asp

As a disruptor, clean energy faces consistent opposition from incumbents. War rages on via backroom public policy fights, lobbyists and think tanks. Governments and regulators, at both state and federal levels, have considerable power to shape the power landscape through policy, taxes, fees, regulations, and tariffs. In the United States, we've seen recent White House influence in this space. For example, in December 2018 the acting administrator of the Environmental Protection Agency, Andrew Wheeler, announced a repeal of regulations put in place by President Obama aimed at reducing carbon dioxide emissions from coal-fired power plants. The EPA claimed to be promoting "clean coal," a term used to describe emerging technologies that capture carbon on site from coal plants.

Unfortunately, "clean coal" technology is neither proven nor affordable, and the EPA's proposal sought to eliminate Obama-era carbon capture and storage requirements. In a cynical twist, Wheeler asserted that coal was good because it benefited poor people: "Affordable energy benefits low and middle-income Americans the most, particularly disadvantaged and underserved communities," Wheeler said.[11]

The very sad and infuriating reality is that these marginalized communities (now sometimes referred to as "frontline communities") have been enduring significant health challenges from "affordable" fossil fuels for decades. Corporations have concentrated operations in these areas to the point where black people are 75% more likely to host industrial facilities in their communities compared to the average American.[12]

The health impact from fossil fuels is abysmal. Each year roughly 30,000 people die prematurely from pollution caused by fossil-fuel power plants, which is a number only slightly lower

---

[11] https://earther.gizmodo.com/the-trump-administration-is-spinning-its-latest-pro-coa-1830917422
[12] https://www.naacp.org/wp-content/uploads/2017/11/Fumes-Across-the-Fence-Line_NAACP-and-CATF-Study.pdf

than gun violence or traffic accidents. If you had the opportunity to save everyone from dying in car crashes each year would you do it? Of course, you would - and of course we should do the same for those affected by reckless pollution.

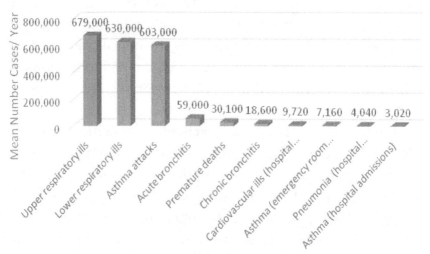

Figure 1: Data from "The Health Costs of Inaction with Respect to Air Pollution," by Pascale Scapecchi, Organization for Economic Cooperation and Development, Environmental Working Papers No. 2.[13]

Even if "clean coal" were possible, it's crazy to continue relying on extracted carbon fuels. Beyond the galling health implications there's simply a finite amount of coal, oil, and gas in the ground. As the population of Earth grows to exceed eight billion people, we need to get smarter about how we create and consume energy.

---

[13] https://www.eesi.org/papers/view/fact-sheet-fossil-fuel-subsidies-a-closer-look-at-tax-breaks-and-societal-costs

Denialism

Much like big tobacco in the mid-20th century, fossil fuel profiteers and their allies engage in underhanded tactics to purposefully mislead the public and maintain the status quo. Climate change deniers tend to fall into three overlapping categories.

The most extreme group asserts that climate change is a hoax perpetrated by scientists with ulterior motives[14]. This is commonly referred to as the global warming conspiracy theory. This position got a boost in November 2009 with the hacking of a server at the Climatic Research Unit (CRU) at the University of East Anglia by an unknown attacker. Thousands of emails and documents were released, which climate deniers seized upon as proof that global warming was a hoax. The story was promoted by deniers including columnist James Delingpole, who popularized the term "Climategate" to describe what he called a scientific conspiracy, with scientists manipulating climate data and attempting to suppress critics.[15]

The second group of climate deniers acknowledge that our climate is changing, but insist it's the result of natural cycles that have been going on for millions of years, and there's nothing we can—or should—do about it. Because humans and other life forms are adaptable, life will go on. The view that climate change is essentially irrelevant was promoted most forcefully by groups like Koch Industries[16], and other organizations with vested interests in continuing carbon pollution. Any government

---

[14] Some deniers in this category have gone so far as to suggest that all other nations are conspiring together, pushing falsehoods to undermine America's greatness. Every other country in the world has signed on to the Paris Climate Accord including Syria and Nicaragua, so yeah, that theory seems perfectly rational...

[15] https://www.telegraph.co.uk/comment/columnists/christopherbooker/6679082/Climate-change-this-is-the-worst-scientific-scandal-of-our-generation.html

[16] A massive global corporation built almost entirely on selling various forms of extracted carbon Founded by David and Charles Koch.

regulations designed to limit the production and consumption of carbon-based energy would negatively impact their bottom line. Measures such as closing coal-fired power plants or increasing efficiency for gasoline-powered motor vehicles, would cost these industries trillions in revenues.

Koch Industries, founded by the Koch brothers (David died in 2019, leaving Charles at the helm), has funded or created a sprawling network of climate-denying organizations and lobbying groups including the Cato Institute (which Charles co-founded in 1977), the American Enterprise Institute, the George C. Marshall Institute, the Reason Foundation, the Heritage Foundation, the Manhattan Institute, and Americans for Prosperity. American's for Prosperity was founded by David Koch himself and spent $40 million on the 2010 Congressional elections alone.[17]

The third group acknowledges climate change—which they call global warming—but insists that it's *beneficial* to the earth and to humanity. This is the position espoused by the Competitive Enterprise Institute, which describes itself as a "non-profit public policy organization dedicated to advancing the principles of limited government, free enterprise, and individual liberty." *Business Insider* has said that Myron Ebell, director of global warming and international environmental policy at CEI, "may be enemy #1 to the current climate change community."[18]

CEI asserts, for example, that "so-called carbon pollution has significant and well documented ecological and food security benefits. That's because rising CO_2 concentrations enable plants to grow faster and larger and use water more efficiently, and warming lengthens agricultural growing seasons."[19]

Professor Richard Tol of Sussex University wrote a chapter in the book *How Much have Global Problems Cost the World?* in which

[17] https://www.campaigncc.org/climate_change/sceptics/funders
[18] https://cei.org/about-cei
[19]https://cei.org/blog/climate-change-fossil-fuels-and-human-well-being?gclid=EAIaIQobChMI2Ma_yOmj5QIVSdyGCh2D6A1pEAAYASAAEgK5QvD_BwE

he argued that the chief benefits of global warming included fewer winter deaths, lower energy costs, better agricultural yields, probably fewer droughts, and maybe richer biodiversity.[20] He claimed it was a "little-known fact" that winter deaths exceed summer deaths even in nations with very warm summers, including Greece, where the daytime winter temperatures average a balmy 58 degrees. Even if this were true, he conveniently ignored research that suggests exposure to sunlight—which in the Northern Hemisphere is more plentiful in the summer months—has a positive psychological effect that has nothing to do with the outside temperature.

Beyond the subversive behavior of their think-tanks the Koch brothers have also asserted publicly that global warming isn't a problem. As reported by *Rolling Stone* David Koch said, "The Earth will be able to support enormously more people because a far greater land area will be available to produce food."[21] Wow, there's so much ridiculousness to unpack with that statement.

It is clear that purposeful actions from denialists have been detrimental to progress on climate. The time is now for traditional media and politicians to do away with both-sidedness when talking about this issue. The science behind human-caused global warming is crystal clear.

Climate Opportunism

Some nations like Russia are realizing strategic opportunities from climate change. The arctic circle has been losing ice for years and many scientists are predicting that arctic summers will

---

[20] https://www.spectator.co.uk/2013/10/carry-on-warming/
[21] https://www.rollingstone.com/politics/politics-lists/whos-to-blame-12-politicians-and-execs-blocking-progress-on-global-warming-149796/charles-and-david-kochceo-and-executive-vp-koch-industries-169023/

consistently be ice-free by the late-2020's or early-2030's[22], opening up strategic shipping routes, military advantages, and mineral exploitation. It's been estimated that the Arctic's untapped mining potential could yield as much as $35 trillion USD.[23]

One thing that most level-headed people can agree on is that global climate change is *disruptive*. It disrupts local environments and the delicate balances that keep climate zones stable and useful for agriculture and other life-sustaining pursuits. When agriculture and water supplies are disrupted, people living in those areas may be forced to leave, abandoning their homes to seek refuge in new places. The result is geopolitical tension, as long-established communities struggle to accommodate those who have been displaced.

Exodus: Climate-Fueled Unrest in Syria

A good example of how climate change can intensify social conflict can be seen in Syria. Since 2011, this ancient nation has been embroiled in a civil war. Among its primary causes are environmental upheaval, particularly the 2007-2010 drought. According to a 2014 report by Peter Gleick in *Advancing Science* entitled, "Water, Drought, Climate Change, and Conflict in Syria," the effects of the drought, including agricultural failure, water shortages, and water mismanagement, displaced rural populations, forcing mass migration to the cities. Agricultural failures affected approximately 1.3 million people living in eastern Syria, with an estimated 800,000 people losing their

---

[22] https://en.wikipedia.org/wiki/Arctic_sea_ice_decline#Observation
[23] https://www.cnbc.com/2019/12/27/russias-dominance-in-the-arctic.html

livelihoods and becoming at risk for malnutrition. During the drought, livestock populations and yields from wheat and barley dropped by 47 percent and 67 percent respectively. Before the drought, 25 percent of Syria's GDP was attributed to agriculture; after 2008, this number dropped to 17 percent.[24]

The United Nations estimated that by late 2011—when the uprising began—between two and three million people were affected, with one million driven into food insecurity. Repeated crop failures triggered the migration of as many as 1.5 million people from rural to urban areas on the outskirts of Syria's major cities of Aleppo, Damascus, Dara'a, Deir ez-Zour, Hama, and Homs.[25] In 2002, the total urban population of Syria had been 8.9 million. By 2010 that number ballooned to 13.8 million—a 50 percent increase.[26]

As Smithsonian.com noted in 2013, between 2003 and 2009 the Gravity Recovery and Climate Experiment (GRACE), a pair of satellites operated by NASA and Germany's aerospace center, measured groundwater usage in Syria, and found that the Tigris-Euphrates Basin—comprising Turkey, Syria, Iraq, and western Iran—was losing water faster than any other place in the world except northern India.[27]

Was the drought a result of climate change? Many scientists believe it was. Researchers analyzed historical precipitation and surface temperatures using data from the University of East Anglia Climatic Research Unit and the two Global Historical Climatology Network (GHCN) stations located closest to Syria's northeastern agricultural region. They found a long-term trend of decreasing rainfall and increasing temperatures in the 20th

---

[24] https://www.climatecenter.pitt.edu/news/drought-syria
[25] Gleick: https://journals.ametsoc.org/doi/full/10.1175/WCAS-D-13-00059.1
[26] https://www.climatecenter.pitt.edu/news/drought-syria

[27]https://www.smithsonianmag.com/innovation/is-a-lack-of-water-to-blame-for-the-conflict-in-syria-72513729/#ViLcBgd47VfoITGz.99

century, which have become especially acute in the last twenty years.

In their report "Climate change in the Fertile Crescent and implications of the recent Syrian drought," Colin P. Kelley and colleagues found the observed drying and warming in the Fertile Crescent "are consistent with model studies of the response to increases in greenhouse gases. Furthermore, model studies show an increasingly drier and hotter future mean climate for the Eastern Mediterranean."[28]

To be sure, there are many reasons why civil war erupted in Syria, including human greed, tribalism, and ruthless political ambition. The unrest formally began on March 15, 2011, when pro-democracy demonstrations erupted in the southern city of Deraa, inspired by the Arab Spring in neighboring countries. Instead of allowing the demonstrations to dissipate, the government of President Bashar al-Assad used deadly force to crush dissent, triggering protests nationwide demanding the president's resignation.

If Syria had not been in the grip of a drought caused in part by human-made climate change, perhaps tensions would have relaxed before lines had been crossed and there was no turning back.

Episode V – the Pentagon Strikes Back

For reasons ranging from sincere beliefs to full-blown self-interest, pro-carbon politicians embrace and disseminate propaganda from climate deniers. Their opinions and legislation serve to muddy the waters, leading much of the public to wonder

---

[28] https://www.pnas.org/content/early/2015/02/23/1421533112

what's accurate. But the vast bureaucracy of the federal government is full of scientists and policy advocates who are professional and non-political and strive for objectivity. Many agencies are very serious about uncovering and confronting threats to our national security, chief among them is the US national defense establishment. Operating on an annual budget approaching $700 billion, the people tasked with defending our nation through our global network of military installations and physical assets want to deal with reality, not fantasy. They're successful at keeping regressive politicians at arm's length—but sadly, that's not always possible.

Even in a highly politicized environment, the defense establishment is beginning to take climate change seriously.

In January 2019, the Pentagon published a study of the climate crisis creatively named the "Report on Effects of a Changing Climate to the Department of Defense," in which Pentagon experts assessed 79 mission assurance priority installations based on their operational role. These installations included Army, Air Force, and Naval bases. The findings showed that 53 of the 79 faced current threats from flooding; 43 of the 79 face current threats from drought, and 36 of the 79 faced current threats from wildfires.

What does this mean? The Pentagon summarized it well: "the effects of a changing climate are a *national security issue* with potential impacts to Department of Defense missions, operational plans, and installations."[29]

Seems pretty bad, right? Well, it might be even worse than the report suggests. The Pentagon's report is the result of a directive from the 2018 National Defense Authorization Act, requiring the

---

[29] Pentagon: https://media.defense.gov/2019/Jan/29/2002084200/-1/-1/1/CLIMATE-CHANGE-REPORT-2019.PDF

Pentagon to produce an "assessment of the significant vulnerabilities from climate-related events in order to identify high risks to mission effectiveness on installations and to operations." The report seems to have been watered down for political reasons. For instance, critics questioned why not *one* Marine Corps Base was included. The report also failed to mention some of the massive storm damage to military installations in 2018. After all, the preceding year's report marked the terror of Hurricane Michael, which caused major damage to all Tyndall Air Force Base buildings, not to mention the destruction wreaked by Hurricane Florence to the Marines' Camp Lejeune.

Sadly, our national defense community is not immune to outside political pressure. The initial climate change roadmap order in 2014 by the Obama Administration was stopped by the incoming Trump administration. In 2016, edits were made to the report that limited the mentions of climate change and its impact on military bases and combat strategy. The 2019 report took steps forward in admitting there was an issue, but upon its release, it received no official public announcement.

Even following the 2019 report released in January of that year, there continues to be a lack of acknowledgment from military planners. As of June 2019, there are reportedly "billions of dollars in damage at bases." Including previous climate-related events earlier that year when, as Leo Shane III wrote, "nearly one-third of Offutt Air Force Base in Nebraska was submerged by floods in the region. Bases in Florida, Nebraska, and North Carolina are still making repairs from when Hurricane Michael made landfall last October."[30]

---

[30] **Shane:** https://www.militarytimes.com/news/pentagon-congress/2019/06/06/the-military-is-being-pulled-deeper-into-the-climate-change-debate/

Miami's Vice

Rising sea levels due to warming water and global ice melting are a threat to hundreds of millions of people living in low-lying coastal areas. A study published in May 2019 in the *Proceedings of the National Academy of Sciences* reports that rising seas could lead to the displacement of 187 million people, as land totaling an area larger than Alaska is lost to the sea. This is a catastrophic climate scenario for nearly every coastal community on Earth.[31]

The urban area of Miami-Dade County, with a population of 2.75 million, is already seeing the effects of rising seas as roads and front yards are awash during high tides. Miami is particularly vulnerable because its underlying bedrock is limestone, which makes the effects of sea-level rise particularly dangerous. "Limestone is very porous, so saltwater can seep up," said Ben Wilson, an environmental scientist, to *The New Yorker*. "We can't just build a wall to keep salt-water out."[32] And along the shoreline, increased salt-water intrusion is causing natural freshwater marshes, which act as coastal barriers against storm surge, to collapse.

As *The New York Times* reported in February 2019, if carbon emissions continue and sea levels respond moderately, by 2100 about 10 percent of Miami will be below the once-a-year coastal flood height, putting trillions of real estate assets at risk.

People whose livelihoods are threatened by climate change—and particularly rising sea levels—don't have time for political chicanery. They need substantive plans, and they need to get to work.

---

[31] https://www.pnas.org/content/116/23/11195
[32] https://www.newyorker.com/news/news-desk/miami-faces-an-underwater-future

In Miami-Dade County, the local government is responding. The Office of Resilience minces no words: "Climate change and sea-level rise are long term stresses that will amplify other issues in our county from intensifying storm events and hurricanes to impacting human health and social vulnerability."

These words are backed by actions. Mitigation is a countywide effort; as the city's Office of Resilience says, "Climate change mitigation refers to efforts to limit the magnitude of climate change by reducing emissions of greenhouse gases (GHG). Through the Compact of Mayors, Mayor Carlos Gimenez has committed the County to reducing our community-wide GHG emissions and regularly reporting our progress. The County is working toward this commitment by targeting the largest sources of GHG emissions—buildings and transportation. This effort includes policies and programs to reduce emissions through energy and water conservation, increased efficiency, and decreased fossil fuel use."[33]

If only we had such clarity and decisiveness from political leaders in Washington, D.C.

Speaking of Washington, our nation's capital is not immune to rising sea levels. According to Climate Central, 1,350 acres of the city's land lies less than six feet above the high tide line. This zone includes $4.6 billion in property value and 1,400 people in 400 homes. If you expand the zone to include land below the ten-foot-high tide line, these figures jump to $9 billion in property value and 4,833 people residing in 1,900 homes.[34]

A three-foot rise in sea level—a conservative number calculated solely on the current rate of melting of the ice sheets in Antarctica—would sink much of Gravelly Point, the Tidal Basin,

---

[33] https://www.miamidade.gov/mayor/climate-change-and-sea-level-rise.asp
[34] http://sealevel.climatecentral.org/research/reports/washington-dc-and-the-surging-sea

the northern bit of Joint Base Anacostia-Bolling, and the road around East Potomac Park.[35]

If climate-change-denying lawmakers see the Potomac sloshing around the base of Capitol Hill they'd likely still chalk it up to chance or religious symbolism. But maybe, just maybe, that reality would be too hard to ignore, either way, it'd be too late.

---

[35] https://www.washingtonian.com/2016/03/31/these-maps-show-what-washington-will-look-like-when-antarctica-melts/

2. The Case for a Green Recovery

2020 will be known as the year of adaptation and empowerment. The first half bookended by a worldwide and US-centric pandemic on one side and the culmination of a centuries-long battle for justice on the other, everyone and everything has changed.

No one can remain silent or idle in this time of upheaval. The "Greatest Generation" rose from the ashes to defeat fascism, but fell short of providing access to the American dream for everyone. 18th-century Patriots fought and won independence, but did so while exploiting indigenous people and slave labor. Now is the time for Millennials, Gen Z, and everyone drawn toward a more environmentally and socially just future to link arms. We can also rise from the ashes, and win independence, but do so on a platform that lifts everyone. It's a promise we can and must deliver on.

Hearing the names George Floyd and Breonna Taylor, or Covid19 doesn't immediately conjure images of the climate crisis. Warming and pollution may not seem like aggravating factors, but they are, among many, but by no means the least significant. Climate's impacts are felt in ways that are so asymmetrical that it's inherently difficult to connect the dots. Below the surface, health and social tensions have been rising steadily, culminating in the current breaking point.

While the Coronavirus has and will continue to have a tremendous impact on the entire global population, many have failed to recognize its connection to the climate crisis. With global economies shut down, less and less energy was being used and pollutants were reduced at an unfathomable rate. Could the whole situation be nature's response to our collective environmental failure? Is the epidemic forcing us to realize the true gravity of caring for our environment?

The Climate-Fueled Corona Crisis

COVID19's origin story has been credibly traced to so-called wet markets in Asia. While the exact time and place of an outbreak could never be predicted, preconditions certainly could. As the population balloons beyond 8 billion people, humanity has stretched itself into areas where contact with wild species is inevitable. We've also destroyed habitat so that our interaction with exotic animals at society's fringes is near certain. Wild creatures that harbor viruses like COVID19 are engaging with people. Wet markets like we see in East Asia, create the opportunity for disease to spread from one species to another.

Scientists have cautioned us about the Coronavirus, and they've cautioned us about the climate crisis. We've witnessed the dangers of not listening to doctors and scientists regarding this virus, and we shouldn't wait to heed warnings about destabilizing the Earth's ecosystems.

The primary message is that rather than seeing Coronavirus as a retaliation of nature against humanity, we should take notice of what happens when humanity fails to address critical issues when we have the knowledge and power to react. If we continue to deny the climate crisis or respond with incrementalism, we will continue to face similar challenges like COVID19, and far worse.

There are obvious parallels between COVID denialism and continued climate change denialism. It took the federal government and President Trump months to understand and address the real threat of Coronavirus. Even when the impacts of the disease became very clear in the United States, many tried to dampen its severity - watering down facts as a means to serve self-interests.

This is not at all dissimilar to messaging around the climate crisis. Despite undeniable proof, many have cherry-picked facts or flat out lied to prevent any perception of consensus. The key takeaway from Coronavirus is that suppressing facts and not listening to science will lead to prolonged and unnecessary hardships.

Disruption caused by Coronavirus has been all-encompassing. It's insensitive to say that anything "good" has come from the pandemic, but many have acknowledged the environmental upshots from a global lockdown, shelter-in-place orders, and reduced industry operations. Martha Henriques from BBC sums it up best stating, "It is all aimed at controlling the spread of Covid-19, and hopefully reducing the death toll. But all this change has also led to some unexpected consequences. As industries, transport networks, and businesses have closed down, it has brought a sudden drop in carbon emissions."

Specific data gathered by the BBC shows the incredible environmental impact of the pandemic spanning all over the globe. Compared with this time last year, levels of pollution in New York have reduced by nearly 50%. In China, emissions fell 25% at the start of the year as people were instructed to stay at home. Factories closed and coal use declined by 40% at China's six largest power plants.

In areas like Los Angeles and Shanghai people enjoyed sightlines normally oppressed by smog. Wildlife ventured back into urban areas; fleetingly reclaiming territory ceded to human development.

It's unknown what the long-term impacts of COVID-19 will actually look like. One thing that is clear: the topic is sure to remain top of mind for years to come. Our lives will be impacted for years to come and they may not ever be the same. Many hope the climate crisis issue won't fade into obscurity.

In late September 2019 the Fridays for Future school strikes, led by the immutable Greta Thunberg, nearly 6 million protestors took to the streets. The environmental movement was finally gaining momentum. As the virus and American politics have clawed away at those gains it's time to take a stand and demand action.

One thing COVID-19 has shown the world, albeit to varying degrees of success, is that a globally coordinated crisis response is possible with strong leadership. The blueprint of mass mobilization to solve big issues is one that should not be soon forgotten. We have the ability to tackle problems together, and similar efforts will be needed to solve Climate Change.

Environmental Justice - I Can't Breathe

On May 25th, 2020 the world changed with the murder of George Floyd at the hands of Minneapolis Police. As a Twin Cities resident who spent decades between Minneapolis and St. Paul, I couldn't forecast that the tragedy would happen, but the fact that it did, in my hometown, wasn't surprising.

As a person of color living just a few miles from his death, the injustice was especially horrific. I'm not black but have experienced prejudice in my life, and empathize deeply with the Black Lives Matter movement. What's happened in Minnesota is the culmination of vast racial inequality, nearly the worst in the nation.

Many more-qualified scholars have written on this subject with eloquence and power. Similar to other areas of the country, neo-segregation tactics in the Twin Cities have prevented upward economic mobility for communities of color. School map realignment, polluter exploitation, and generational under-investment all play a role. Tensions in under-resourced communities can boil over into desperation when we're faced with crises like COVID19.

The clean energy industry certainly does not have all the answers. In fact, diversity has been a big problem for most green organizations. So, we must listen. But we also must lead with our actions. Renewable energy promoters have the tendency to glance over details of exactly how we benefit society in social ways. Instead, we need to actively attract talent from under-resourced communities and invest in developing projects in those areas.

My company has done a passable job of this, but even I can admit that it's not nearly enough. When we built a community solar project in 2018 at Shiloh Temple Church in North Minneapolis, we had a workforce development plan that led directly to several new hires. But access to reliable transportation, background restrictions, and inflexibility with labor unions prevented their long-term success. It's an urgent reminder of the systemic barriers to racial justice that still exist today.

We need to break down these invisible walls. The livelihood of these communities means more than carrying an electrical card or having a spotless record. The clean energy movement can't afford to leave anyone behind, especially when the literal future of our planet is on the line.

As our black and brown neighborhoods across America continue to face real threats to safety from the same systems that exist to protect them, it's clear that there can be no climate justice without racial justice. These are our colleagues, partners, clients, friends, and family - the statistics are unacceptable.

Blacks and Hispanics are much more likely to live downstream from coal plants or near hazardous waste sites. In 2015 the death rate from asthma for black children was 10 times higher than the rate for white children. Exposure to more air pollution is one of the primary factors.

BIPOC (Black, Indigenous, People of Color) neighborhoods in the US are breathing 38% more nitrogen oxide on average than white communities.

A study from Harvard University, updated on April 5, confirmed a direct correlation between long-term exposure to air pollution and a higher risk of death from coronavirus. Those suffering from respiratory illness are at a much higher risk of death. For areas in which we have information, blacks are 2.1 times as likely to die from this disease, according to data compiled by the Associated Press.

In a recent interview with Yale360[36], University of Maryland Environmental Health Scientist Sacoby Wilson gave context to some of the major issues facing under-resourced frontline communities amidst this crisis:

Environmental regulations in this country, they're not color blind. If the laws and regulations were enforced fairly across all racial-ethnic groups, we wouldn't have environmental injustice. Why do we have communities with more sources of pollution? Well, that could be because those communities don't have a strong political voice. In many cases, in white, higher-income communities, you have more political power because of your economic power. So, this NIMBY-ism, 'Not In My Backyard,' can stop an incinerator, stop a landfill, stop a highway from being built in those neighborhoods. Whereas, a lower-wealth community of color, because they don't have the economic capital which drives their political capital, they don't have the capacity to prevent the siting of those types of things in their community.

---

[36] https://e360.yale.edu/features/connecting-the-dots-between-environmental-injustice-and-the-coronavirus

There's a link between race and class in this country. In many communities of color, industrial developments are seen as economic opportunities. So, you are bringing in these industries that may provide jobs, but what you get instead is the pollution that is produced. And so, there's a cost/benefit analysis that doesn't really look at the true costs of, say, bringing a power plant into a community. The true cost-accounting of bringing a highway into a community, or a landfill, a refinery, a factory, a chemical facility, or a paper mill. What happens is you have these environmental externalities, the pollution impacts, from the facility. And then, you have the health impacts. We have a lot of black and brown communities, a lot of Native American communities, a lot of immigrant communities that are basically sacrifice zones because they are the dumping grounds for these pollution-intensive facilities.

Part of the reason why folks have a higher risk of mortality when you have a Covid-19 infection and if you have asthma, you have reduced lung capacity. Your lungs are not as healthy as someone who has not been exposed to these pollutants. One reason African Americans or Latinos are dying from Covid-19 at rates higher than the other populations is because of underlying health conditions like diabetes, heart disease, and asthma. But your diet and behavior is driven by your context. If you only have fast food in your neighborhood, and you don't have access to a grocery store, what are you going to eat? If you don't have access to healthcare in your neighborhood and you don't have insurance, what are you going to do? And, when you do have access, it may be poor-quality access. Context matters. Place matters. I want to emphasize that point.

As governments debate what a post-COVID and post-George Floyd recovery looks like, it only makes sense that significant dollars go toward addressing environmental justice. Investment in underserved communities with strategies such as lowering vehicle emissions, replacing coal plants with clean energy, and increasing ownership opportunities of those assets must be examined. Plans will be developed over the coming years and stakeholder involvement will be essential to creating impacts that last. So, let's open the doors to those who typically haven't had a seat at the table, avoid dictating solutions, and instead co-create a more equitable future.

Massive grassroots organizing and peaceful protests have sprouted up across America and the globe. Just as COVID has taught us about coordinated leadership and shared sacrifices for the greater good, the aftermath of George Floyd's death has ignited the raw spirit of activism; a desire to build a stronger future together in support of black lives. Those emotions, pointed conversations, organized assemblies, are important tools for the climate movement to understand and learn from. How to channel intense emotions toward a focused call for change, in ways that resonate and move people to action is critical.

Condensing these issues into a subchapter feels woefully insufficient. But if we don't first acknowledge the problems and their connectedness to the broader picture then we can't take any meaningful steps forward as a society and as an industry. A statement from Al Gore's Climate Reality Project in June 2020 summarized it best:

What we do know is this: For us in the climate movement, this fight must be our fight. The fight for justice for George Floyd must be our fight. The fight against white supremacy and systemic racism that also took the lives of Ahmaud Arbery, Breonna Taylor, Freddie Gray, Philando Castile, Alton Sterling, Sandra Bland, Laquan McDonald, Tamir Rice, and so many others must be our fight.

We cannot fight for a better future while looking past the real evils plaguing the present. There cannot be climate justice without racial justice. End of story.

The statement went on:

The ties go beyond the philosophical. As the climate crisis deepens and drives us toward ecological collapse, those who suffer the most will inevitably be the same people of color who for decades have seen their dreams deferred by political neglect and a fundamental lack of concern in the halls of power.

We can already see the same process happening in the COVID-19 pandemic as the factors creating this disproportionate impact – the coal plants and industrial plants overwhelmingly located in minority neighborhoods and poisoning the air, lack of proper housing and access to resources, inadequate infrastructure and little support in recovery – are also creating a tragedy where black Americans are three times more likely to die from the virus than whites.

This is our fight. Which means that justice has to be at the heart of everything we do. We can't celebrate the incredible progress of clean energy alternatives like wind and solar without fighting to ensure they're accessible to everyone. We can't work to end the fossil fuel economy without giving the families and communities it supports a better option and green jobs with a future. It's either all of us or none of us.

Most of all, we have to make room at the table and give up our privilege – if we have it – to actually listen to the voices that have so long been ignored or left out entirely. No matter how hard or painful it may be. Native tribes and indigenous peoples. Activists of color and poor families who know what it's like to watch climate-fueled floods take your home and feel the silence of no government agency coming to your rescue. Young people watching bureaucrats congratulate each other while their future slips away.

As climate activists, this is our fight. The fight for justice and an end to white supremacy. The fight to solve the climate crisis and together build the world we want. The fight to simply exist. The fight for dignity and real freedom for all. The fight to breathe.

So, let's get to work. All of us.

The Answer = Clean Energy Technology

Clean energy can and should be the focal point of economic recovery efforts in 2021 and beyond. Wind, solar, electrification, and energy efficiency projects create jobs, bolster rural and urban economies, and can transform the social inequities made glaringly transparent in 2020.

A series of studies released in April 2020 by E2 and BW Research showed that clean energy jobs had grown 10.2% year over year since 2015; one of the fastest-growing sectors in the U.S. But like the rest of the post-pandemic economy, clean energy needs a stimulus. According to the same research, the sector lost more than 106,000 jobs in March – erasing all gains made in 2019.

Policymakers should look to a policy like the American Recovery and Reinvestment Act of 2009 as a blueprint. The ARRA provided grants in lieu of tax credits so that businesses could invest even if their tax liabilities were low or nonexistent. In 2010 our company, IPS Solar, helped a local hardware store and a nursery in the rural Minnesota community of Lester Prairie install projects with the help of these grants, which lowered their bills and boosted our business. According to the White House Council of Economic Advisors, the ARRA helped support 900,000 clean energy jobs from 2009 to 2015. And the initial boost worked. As the solar industry ramped up, costs declined significantly; compared to 2010, solar panels today are about 89% more cost-effective and efficiency has improved considerably.

Bridging the Political Divide

In these times of divisiveness, especially surrounding the climate issue, there's only one topic that has the power to unite us. Renewable energy is loved by Americans on both sides of the spectrum. 2019 poll results from the Yale Program for Climate Change Communication[37] surveyed nearly 1,000 registered voters in the United States and found that 95 percent of Democrats and 71 percent of Republicans were supportive of policies requiring utilities to adopt 100 percent clean energy standards by 2050. About half of all respondents were willing to pay more on their utility bills for it. More results are telling of America's love for green power:

A majority of Americans (58%) – including three in four Democrats (75%) – think policies intended to transition from fossil fuels to clean, renewable energy will improve economic growth and create new jobs. Only 18% of Americans – and 7% of Democrats – think such policies will reduce growth and jobs. More Republicans think such a transition will improve economic growth (39%) than reduce it (31%).

Americans' most important reasons to support a transition to 100% clean, renewable energy are reducing water pollution (75%), reducing air pollution (74%), and providing a better life for our children and grandchildren (72%).

About seven in ten Americans (71%; including 87% of Democrats and 51% of Republicans) think clean energy should be a "high" or "very high" priority for the president and Congress. Very few Americans (7%, including 3% of Democrats and 11% of Republicans) think it should be a "low" priority.

A majority of Americans (61%) – including about eight in ten Democrats (79%) – think that if all nations switch to 100% clean,

---

[37] https://climatecommunication.yale.edu/publications/energy-in-the-american-mind-december-2018/2/

renewable energy by 2050, it will be "moderately" or "very" effective at limiting global warming.

These findings are something politicians should get behind as federal and state governments draft policy to support our economic recovery.

Helping Farm Communities in Times of Need

Clean energy helps rural communities by providing new tax revenue for local governments, aiding in its aforementioned popularity across the country. In Colfax, Illinois, a small town of only 1,000 people, new wind projects increased the property tax base from $61 million in 2006 to $102 million in 2008, helping the city to weather the worst of the Great Recession. Mower County in southern Minnesota has received $19 million in wind taxes since 2004, according to the Minnesota Department of Revenue. In 2019, wind lowered the county's tax levy by nearly 3 percent. For the Red Wing School District, a 2016 community solar project developed and constructed by IPS is projected to save local taxpayers over $6 million.

As farmers and landowners have endured record low crop prices and other negative impacts from the current trade wars, renewables can offer a much-needed reprise. 2019 farm bankruptcies were up 20% from 2018 to their highest level in 8 years, capping a dismal stretch in which the bankruptcy rate has increased in each of the past five years. Many family farmers have retired, willingly and unwillingly, and sold their land to larger conglomerates, concentrating operations into fewer and fewer corporations.

Even substantial federal farm bailouts have done little to stem the tide. According to the US Department of Agriculture, nearly *one-third* of projected farm revenue dollars in 2019 came from government aid and tax-payer subsidized commodity insurance payments. *One-third.*

Land leases for renewable energy can be generous, and mean the difference between sinking and staying afloat. Wind and solar developers pay quite a bit more than market rates to farmers for use of their land.

In Kansas, wind lease payments to farmers are $15 million to $20 million per year, according to the American Wind Energy Association. Nationally, it's $250 million. Wind turbines require only a modest amount of land at their bases, about the size of a two-car garage. Landowners that host wind turbines can expect to receive $3,000 to $7,000 per year per turbine. Neighbors close enough to these developments can earn substantial "good neighbor" payments.

Solar farms also provide good revenue for farmers. In many cases, farmers receive more than $1,000 per acre per year, which can be 5 to 10 times more than what they receive for agriculture leases. The other benefit to solar leases is that farmers can often help choose where to site the projects on their property. If a project doesn't utilize the entire parcel, panels can be located on the least productive land.

A 2020 USA Today article[38] focused on wind development in rural America interviewed Tom Cunningham, a Kansan who'd been farming an area between Glasco and Concordia for 40 years. The income from leasing his land to the Meridian Way Wind Farm has made an enormous difference:

Before the wind turbines, things were rough, [Cunningham] recalled. Depending on the national and international economy, some years he broke even, some years he made money and, for more years than he cares to think about, he was on the edge. He had to

---

[38]https://www.usatoday.com/story/news/nation/2020/02/16/wind-energy-can-help-american-farmers-earn-money-avoid-bankruptcy/4695670002/

take a job in town to make ends meet and for a time was what he calls "functionally bankrupt."

"This isn't money that other people would think is very much," he said. "But it made an enormous difference to us."

Land Stewardship

Many clean energy opponents decry the conversion of "prime agriculture" land to fields of photovoltaics, but the area required for substantial power generation is insignificant. Minnesota has 25.5 million acres of farmland[39], equivalent to 39,870.28 square miles. According to the Department of Energy's National Renewable Energy Laboratory (NREL), 1 megawatt of solar requires 8.9 acres of land[40], a number that is steadily declining as the efficiency of solar panels improves. According to a recent study by the Minnesota Department of Commerce in order for the state to achieve a 10% solar standard roughly 6 gigawatts of solar is needed, which would require roughly 53,400 acres, only 0.2% of farmland. To reach 100% solar the state would only use 2% of farmland.

There are restorative and environmental benefits to replacing farmland with solar. Rather than laying ground cover like gravel, many developers are deploying pollinator-friendly seed mixes to keep plant growth heights low, and manageable for solar project operators. This seeding also increases vital habitat for bees and butterflies. Solar sites are not traditionally farmed so they avoid common monoculture pitfalls like excessive pesticide use.

Farmers are already paid to conserve land under programs like Minnesota's Conservation Reserve Program otherwise known as CRP. Through CRP, the USDA Farm Services Agency

---

[39]https://www.nass.usda.gov/Publications/AgCensus/2017/Full_Report/Volume_1,_Chapter_1_State_Level/Minnesota/st27_1_0001_0001.pdf

[40] https://www.nrel.gov/docs/fy13osti/56290.pdf

pays farmers to take land out of agricultural production for a period of time. According to an agency factsheet "in return for establishing long-term, resource-conserving covers, FSA provides annual rental payments ... the per-acre annual rental rate may not exceed \$300." For comparison and as alluded to earlier, solar developers are paying up to \$1,200 or more per acre per year. Currently, 1,000,000 acres are enrolled in Minnesota. From an economics standpoint, it would be much more efficient to have private companies pay farmers rates up to 4 times the \$300 CRP maximum, and decrease government subsidies underwritten by taxpayers.

Solar is a temporary land use, once projects have run their course and contracts with utilities have expired it's easy to bring the land back to its original condition. Project owners are often required to post bond security so there are dollars available to restore a property back to its original condition. Steel racking can be dismantled and recycled and panels, as alluded to in Chapter 7: Lifecycle Costs, can have a second life or be refined into new products.

Solar Beer and Apiaries

One of the tastier upshots of combining solar with pollinator-friendly habitat has been the advent of solar farm honey and beer infusions. Many project owners allow beekeepers to install apiaries at the boundaries of their solar sites. Solar developers love pollinator habitat because it often creates a better narrative for local permitting and provides manageable, low-height growth around the panels. Beekeepers have peace of mind that the areas in which they install their hives will be free from pesticides and other harmful chemicals. The resulting honey has found its way

Apiary adjacent to IPS's community solar project near St. Cloud, MN (Photo Credit: National Renewable Energy Labs)

into microbreweries and distilleries across the country, creating beer, cider, and cocktail infusions. James Beard Award-winning chef Gavin Kaysum added solar farm honey desserts to his seasonal menu at Spoon and Stable in Minneapolis.

Rob Davis, director of the Center for Pollinators in Energy at non-profit Fresh Energy[41], has become a national leader in this space and is credited with facilitating the first collaboration between solar farm honey and microbrewing. His team has developed solar farm vegetation programs for more than 3,500 acres of projects in 10 states. In a 2019 article with Craft Brewing Business[42] Davis explained the opportunity and process of growing a deliciously audacious idea into reality:

"Whenever a solar farm is built on arable land, we want to make sure that we make productive use of that land. We want solar farms treated like rich soil that we're borrowing from our grandkids, who will be inheriting it after that solar asset hits its end of life in 30 or 40 years."

"As we scale-up this practice — pairing pollinator-friendly solar farms with beekeeping — we have to keep the use of the product in mind as well," Davis said. "An ideal solution benefits the solar company, the energy buyer, the landscaper, the beekeeper, the brewer, and the restaurateur.

"56 Brewing's use of honey from a flowering solar farm in Solarama Crush points the direction to a fun future with clean energy and sustainable agricultural and ecological systems — a practice Fresh Energy is encouraging."

"Nobody has ever sampled honey from a coal-fired power plant. But you can bring solar farm honey to a permit hearing and hand out samples to everyone and half the people are going back for more. Beer is broadly bipartisan and supported."

"There's a lot of big and small cities throughout the country that have these incredibly ambitious renewable energy goals. It's a great opportunity for brewers to lean forward and explore how

---

[41] Full disclosure - I am a board member of Fresh Energy.
[42] https://www.craftbrewingbusiness.com/featured/this-is-the-beers-knees-how-56-brewings-solarama-crush-includes-the-sun-as-a-key-ingredient/

they can be part of supporting that vision. The key social lubricant in what we do is collaboration."

Since the launch of 56 Brewing's Solarama Crush in 2018, Voodoo Brewing in Pennsylvania, Oregon's Caldera Brewery, and Wisconsin's Driftless Brewing have all tapped the power of solar farm honey. Fresh Energy's most recent collaboration is a beer made with 'sunny' honey by the Alchemist in Vermont.

IPS has had the very good fortune of participating in solar's beerification phenomena. In 2018 honey harvested near our community solar projects in Central Minnesota provided substance for Milk & Honey Cider's *Solar Sweet Farm Cider*.[43] The local PBS station even did an expose about solar farm honey and the brewing community. In one of the stranger and more gratifying twists in my career, that special went on to win a Midwest Regional Emmy Award.

---

[43] We've hosted kegs at our offices seasonally, as available.

3: The Rise of Renewables

"Exploration is the engine that drives innovation. Innovation drives economic growth. So let's all go exploring."

– Edith Widder, American oceanographer, marine biologist, and the co-founder, CEO, and senior scientist at the Ocean Research & Conservation Association.

"Renewable energy is a clear winner when it comes to boosting the economy and creating jobs."

– Tom Steyer, businessman and candidate for US president in 2020.

Despite a mixed political environment, the business climate for clean energy technology has been improving rapidly. Prices are coming down, technology is advancing, and everyday working people are embracing the ideas of electric cars and solar panels on the roofs of their homes. They see renewables as a way to save money, become more energy independent while doing some good for the environment.

As an industry, renewable technologies, with the exception of traditional biomass, may be referred to as "modern renewables." According to OurWorldinData.org, the most popular modern renewables are hydropower, solar, wind, geothermal, and modern biofuel production.

Solar photovoltaics (PV)—the conversion of light into electricity using semiconducting materials that exhibit the photovoltaic effect—and wind are now mainstream options in the power sector, with an increasing number of countries generating more than 20 percent of their electricity with solar PV and wind.

Renewable energy production data is measured in terawatt-hours per year and can be viewed across a range of countries and regions. According to data compiled by researchers Hannah Ritchie and Max Rose[44], total clean energy production has grown by 6-fold over the last 50 years. Recently, and most impressively, wind and solar have been on an absolute tare since the turn of the century. From 2000 to 2018 wind has increased roughly 40-fold from 31.42 terawatt-hours (TWh) annually to 1,270 TWh. Solar, barely a blip in 2000 at 1.13 TWh has exploded to over 584 TWh, a 550-fold increase!

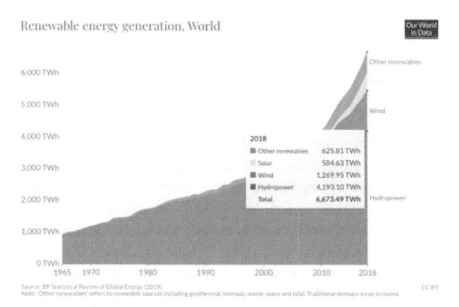

Renewable energy generation, World

2018	
Other renewables	625.81 TWh
Solar	584.63 TWh
Wind	1,269.95 TWh
Hydropower	4,193.10 TWh
Total	6,673.49 TWh

Source: BP Statistical Review of Global Energy (2019)
Note: 'Other renewables' refers to renewable sources including geothermal, biomass, waste, wave and tidal. Traditional biomass is not included.

CC BY

---

[44] Hannah Ritchie and Max Roser (2020) - "Renewable Energy". *Published online at OurWorldInData.org.* Retrieved from: 'https://ourworldindata.org/renewable-energy' [Online Resource]

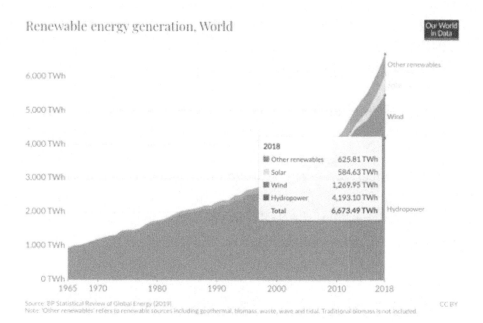

Renewable energy generation, World

2018

Other renewables	625.81 TWh
Solar	584.63 TWh
Wind	1,269.95 TWh
Hydropower	4,193.10 TWh
Total	6,673.49 TWh

Source: BP Statistical Review of Global Energy (2019)
Note: 'Other renewables' refers to renewable sources including geothermal, biomass, waste, wave and tidal. Traditional biomass is not included.

CC BY

This battle is just beginning. While we're making significant advances in the development and deployment of clean energy, global carbon emissions are still increasing. Data from the *Renewables Global Status Report* (GSR), released annually by the Renewable Energy Policy Network for the 21st Century (REN21, a think tank) shows that global carbon emissions were up 1.7 percent in 2018. Globally, subsidies to fossil fuel companies were up 11 percent between 2016 and 2017, reaching $300 billion a year[45] - roughly twice as much in subsidies as clean energy.

So, what impact are modern renewables having? A big one. There are a lot of positive data points associated with trending green energy initiatives. David Roberts at Vox suggested "the shift in the electricity sector has effectively become unstoppable. Globally, more renewable energy capacity has been installed than

---

[45] Roberts: https://www.vox.com/energy-and-environment/2019/6/18/18681591/renewable-energy-china-solar-pv-jobs

new fossil fuel and nuclear capacity combined, for four years running. Some 181 GW of new renewables capacity was installed in 2018; it now makes up more than one-third of global installed power capacity. These are mainstream power sources, here to stay."[46]

Even with the advent of new and better technology, many argue that there's simply an upper limit on what intermittent wind and solar resources can provide. This argument totally ignores advances in energy storage and smart grid technology which is on a similar exponential path. NREL recently completed a study showing that the U.S. can generate nearly all of its electricity from renewable energy by 2050.[47]

Clean Energy = Jobs + Economic Development

Renewables aren't just a strategy to reduce CO_2 emissions and help slow climate change—it's become an economic engine and leading job creator. According to a recent National Solar Jobs Census published by *The Solar Foundation*, in the United States, the industry creates more jobs than any other sector. According to the census, solar energy adds jobs 17 times faster than the overall economy. For example, in 2010, there were 93,000 jobs in solar. By 2018, the industry employed over 242,000 people. During that year, one in every fifty new jobs was in the solar industry.

In 2018, solar jobs increased in 29 states, including many states with emerging solar markets such as Florida, Minnesota, Texas, and New York State.[48]

---

[46] Roberts: Ibid.
[47] NREL: https://www.nrel.gov/analysis/re-futures.html
[48] https://www.thesolarfoundation.org/national/

The overall renewable energy sector is growing as well. EDF.org reported that as of January 2018 the U.S. renewable energy sector employed 777,000 people, about the same number as the telecommunications industry. Bioenergy remained the largest employer, while the solar industry was second.

The most *rapid* renewable energy job growth has come from the solar and wind sectors, which from 2016 to 2017 rose by 24.5 percent and 16 percent, respectively. In thirty states, including the District of Columbia, solar and wind energy jobs outnumber coal and gas jobs.

Advanced energy jobs, which includes energy efficiency and other green technology as well as renewables, grew more than twice as fast as the overall economy from 2017 to 2018. At 3.5 million jobs, advanced energy employs more U.S. workers than retail stores (3 million), twice as many as hotels and motels (1.7 million), and more than three times as many as the coal and oil industries combined (1 million).[49] That's more than the number of people employed as registered nurses and just shy of those working as school teachers.[50]

According to the same report, energy efficiency made up more than half of the new energy jobs created in 2017, adding 67,000 jobs—growing at about twice the national rate. Overall, energy efficiency employed 2.25 million people. Meanwhile, solar power employed 350,000 workers, while wind power employed 107,000. For comparison, the coal industry employs 160,000 workers, less than a quarter as many Americans as the renewable energy industry.[51,52]

---

[49] According to the Bureau of Labor Statistics (retail and hotel/motel) and USEER (coal and oil). https://www.aee.net/articles/advanced-energy-gains-125000-jobs-in-2018-growing-twice-as-fast-as-u.s.-employment-overall
[50] https://static1.squarespace.com/static/5a98cf80ec4eb7c5cd928c61/t/5c7f3708fa0d6036d7120d8f/1551849054549/USEER+2019+US+Energy+Employment+Report.pdf
[51] https://www.edf.org/energy/clean-energy-jobs
[52] These numbers reflect our experience at IPS Solar. In 2013, we had just four employees. Today, we have over forty employees, and that number continues to grow at a constant rate.

The clean energy industry also generates hundreds of billions in economic activity and is expected to continue to grow rapidly in the coming years, according to the U.S. Department of Energy. There is tremendous economic opportunity for the countries that invent, manufacture, and export clean energy technologies.[53]

In 2017, global clean energy investment totaled $333.5 billion, the second-highest amount ever recorded, according to Bloomberg New Energy Finance (NEF). This is almost five times the $70.9 billion invested in clean energy in 2006. China was on top with $132.6 billion, and the U.S. came in second at $56.9 billion.[54] For some perspective 2017 clean energy investment was identical to the EU's GDP output from agriculture.

In an estimate that would have been shocking ten years ago, Bloomberg NEF recently projected that $10 trillion will be invested in new clean power infrastructure.[55] Money supporting new wind, solar, and battery development around the globe will continue to rise. The $10 trillion number is very likely to be revised upwards, many times over.

Health & the Green Revolution

Beyond jobs and saving the glaciers, clean energy has real and impactful health benefits. Significantly reducing emissions in the energy and transport sectors could prevent almost 300,000 early deaths caused by air pollution each year in the U.S. by 2030, according to a Duke University study.[56] That's equivalent to saving the entire population of Madison, Wisconsin, *each year*. A staggering number.

---

[53] US Dept. Energy: https://www.energy.gov/science-innovation/clean-energy
[54] https://data.bloomberglp.com/professional/sites/24/BNEF-Clean-Energy-Investment-Trends-2018.pdf
[55] https://about.bnef.com/blog/solar-wind-batteries-attract-10-trillion-2050-curbing-emissions-long-term-will-require-technologies/
[56] https://www.nature.com/articles/nclimate2935

Fossil fuel emissions cause nearly $5 billion in U.S. medical costs associated with premature births, according to a study by the New York University School of Medicine.[57] Continued reliance on coal will cost 52,000 American lives per year, according to a study by the Michigan Technological University.[58]

Pollution is bad, I hope that's obvious. Simple luxuries available to western societies, including clean air and water, are not afforded to most of the global population. Creating a healthier world will mean a more equitable future for all.

Your Reason for Waking Up

If the information in these first few chapters inspires you, then you're likely on the right path. True meaning for many people revolves around doing what you love, the essence of which is commonly known as your *why*. For me, defeating the climate crisis is my defining *why*, and it is likely similar for many clean energy professionals. In the preface I provided some background as to why this cause and my journey are so personal. It's typically in those vulnerabilities that people identify what's truly important, and I encourage you to explore those areas within yourself.

Evan Hynes, the founder and director of Climatebase[59] and thought leader in cleantech professional development might be the first to admit that it took several journeys (both figuratively and literally) to discover his *why*. Before we get into that story a quick plug for his organization – Climatebase is a web platform mobilizing the world's talent to solve the climate crisis, by helping talented jobseekers find high-impact jobs at companies and nonprofits working to address climate change. In the

---

[57] https://ehp.niehs.nih.gov/doi/10.1289/ehp.1510810
[58] ClimateNexus.org:https://climatenexus.org/climate-issues/energy/top-clean-energy-stats-2018/
[59] Formerly Climate.Careers. https://climatebase.org/

organization's words, they're "leveraging employment as a vehicle to drive climate action."

The site partners with organizations advancing climate solutions, as well as research, policy, education, and advocacy for climate action. They support those organizations by helping them attract mission-driven talent.

24 million new climate-impactful jobs will be created by 2030 as a result of addressing the climate crisis, according to the International Labor Organization.[60] Hyne's organization exists to accelerate this critical shift, by building a network for climate solutionists, the individuals and organizations working to address climate change.

Evan graduated college from UC Santa Barbara, and like many in California went to work in the tech world after a brief stint with a large company in the Bay Area he found his way into the start-up community, which was a passion of his. After joining a small team and helping to scale an organization something was still missing.

Like a number of enterprising individuals facing similar moments of truth Hynes decided to take a one-year sabbatical to travel and clear his mind. Travel can be extremely cathartic and perspective-changing.[61] A 2017 Inc.com article by Tanya Hall, CEO of Greenleaf Book Group, put it succinctly:

When you're feeling disengaged or cynical, schedule time off and follow what you're craving. Find a retreat by the ocean if you're stressed, or sign up for rock climbing or scuba diving if you're restless. Fulfilling personal needs can clear your mind to focus on

---

[60] https://www.un.org/sustainabledevelopment/blog/2019/04/green-economy-could-create-24-million-new-jobs/
[61] My mom worked for decades in the travel industry. Some of my favorite memories over the years are those of being with family and friends, experiencing new things and new places. For the same reason, I'm also a huge fan of travelogues as a necessary distraction.

moving forward, and the time away can make you excited to be back in the office.

Sometimes our greatest failures at work stem from the fact that our teams see things the same way. To avoid repeating mistakes and to spark innovation, leaders should test the limits of their own thinking by exploring cultures that think differently.

In Hynes' words, "I was ready to sink teeth into something new. As someone who hasn't been able to compartmentalize, work is so tied to my identity and how I operate. Toward the tail end of my trip, I stopped to visit a former tech co-worker and friend who was working on a regenerative ranging project. His new project centered around working with cattle to manage grazing habits in hopes of reducing greenhouse gas emissions. One night, sitting by the fire he handed me a book called Drawdown."

Drawdown is an influential book by Paul Hawken that explores 100 of the most critical solutions to combating the climate crisis. Sustainable agriculture is certainly one of those opportunities, as is clean energy. "The IPCC report on climate change[62] came out a few months before I came back. **I wasn't shocked by the findings; I was simply terrified.** I have memories of my parents taking me to see An Inconvenient Truth when I was young, and it was scary. I was thinking, wow, this is terrible, but we'll assign our best and brightest to tackle solutions and progress will be made. After a decade, the [IPCC] report made it clear that whatever we had done wasn't enough."

Hynes was winding down his nearly year-long journey which had definitely contributed to his sense of openness. The confluence of perception, messaging, and introspection contributed to his *Aha Moment*, a pivotal juncture that changed

---

[62] https://www.ipcc.ch/sr15/

his mentality and future. "I was in my late 20's, seeing the path that we were on, which was getting worse, and knew climate would be my career calling."

Ikigai

A JAPANESE CONCEPT MEANING "A REASON FOR BEING"

Satisfaction, but feeling of uselessness

What you LOVE

Delight and fullness, but no wealth

PASSION   MISSION

What you are GOOD AT

Ikigai

What the world NEEDS

PROFESSION   VOCATION

Comfortable, but feeling of emptiness

What you can be PAID FOR

Excitement and complacency, but sense of uncertainty

SOURCE: dreamstime   TORONTO STAR GRAPHIC

Originating in feudal Japan, the word "Ikigai" loosely translates to "reason for waking up in the morning." As shown in the Venn diagram above there are four circles representing important elements of our professional lives:

1. What you LOVE
2. What you are GOOD AT
3. What you can be PAID FOR
4. What the world NEEDS

Taking a serious self-assessment of each circle may help lead to a breakthrough moment.

This framework shows that there's further nuance in overlapping areas. For instance, if you love your work, are good at it, and can be paid well for your efforts, but it's not what the world needs, you might have a feeling of satisfaction but uselessness also. Only when focusing on all four areas can you achieve Ikigai.

The reality for many people is that their jobs have been commoditized and productized. We're worker bees, punching the clock simply to cash a paycheck and live our real lives outside of normal business hours. But working can and should be a source of fulfillment. Many in the clean energy industry have found Ikigai in their work.

If you're mission-driven, let it show. Not just on your resume but outside of internships and classes. Go above and beyond. Employers in the climate space are not looking for someone who will simply fill a position, they want someone who is passionate.

For employers, being mission-driven is a huge boost to the bottom-line. According to LinkedIn's 2020 Global Talent Trends report, organizations that rated highly on purposeful mission saw 49% lower attrition than industry averages. The report also links company purpose as a driver for increased employee well-being:

Having a strong organizational purpose makes people feel part of something valuable regardless of their age, rank, or span of control. Social media has heightened the pressure for everyone to be a superstar. Being part of a larger mission helps ease the tension to change the world all by yourself.

According to the data, mission-driven workers are twice as likely to be promoted and half as
likely to leave. For employers, it's important to identify passion as a hiring metric because it directly correlates to increased performance and retention."

For instance, it's never too early to start writing a blog. When Hines worked at Oracle in corporate sales he wanted to join the startup space that continues to thrive in the San Francisco area. In order to break through he'd started a blog and was interviewing startup founders. His real goal was to get a job, and after only three interviews he'd gotten two offers and landed a position with one of them. "It's very critical that young job seekers understand that you'll be good at what you like doing. If you don't like sitting down at a computer and thinking through problems then you probably shouldn't be a software engineer. Success comes from things that you innately enjoy."

4. The Cleantech Ecosystem

"As the saying goes, the Stone Age did not end because we ran out of stones; we transitioned to better solutions. The same opportunity lies before us with energy efficiency and clean energy."

- Steven Chu, Noble-Prize-winning American physicist

"I'd put my money on the sun and solar energy. What a source of power! I hope we don't have to wait until oil and coal run out before we tackle that."

- Thomas Edison, American inventor (1931)

Cleantech is such a broad and all-encompassing term; what does it really mean? What markets exist in this space and what does that mean for prospective job seekers and entrepreneurs? Typically, when people think of clean energy technology most associate solar and wind power as its monolithic and dominant forces. But things are not so cut and dry. As we learned in the previous chapters, hydro actually creates substantially more power than all other renewable energy combined (but that's changing quickly). And there are more worldwide jobs in energy efficiency, the MVP of cleantech than there are in wind or solar.

Likewise, if you're considering a career in this field, you may be unaware of just how diverse the ecosystem actually is. Some technologies may be less sexy or are still in their early stages of development, so correspondingly they get less attention.

This chapter focuses on the overview of cleantech and where it's headed.

Clean energy also encompasses other technology including the Internet of Things (IOT), electrified transportation, and advanced battery technology. All have a role to play in the future of power and we'll review a few of these smaller market segments in this chapter.

Energy Generation

Within cleantech, energy generation is leading the transition in terms of annual investment and deployment. Five types of renewable energy are generated by harnessing natural processes: solar, wind, geothermal, hydro, and ocean or wave technology. These are considered the most sustainable forms of energy.

Two types of renewable energy are produced using mechanical means, rather than by harnessing a natural process: bioenergy and hydrogen.

Solar Photovoltaic Systems

Commonly known as PV, solar photovoltaic technology captures sunlight energy and converts it into electricity. PV has overtaken other types of solar power like solar thermal and concentrating solar power as the future of solar energy.

Semiconductor materials absorb photons, or particles of light, creating a reaction that knocks electrons loose from their atoms, which makes them flow through the semiconductor material and produce energy.

Solar panels are composed of many smaller units called photovoltaic cells. Each photovoltaic cell is a sandwich made up of two layers of semi-conducting material, usually silicon, the same material used in microelectronics. The top layer has a negative charge, while the bottom layer has a positive charge. This creates an electric field in the space between, not unlike a magnetic field produced by the opposite poles of a magnet.

When a photon of sunlight knocks free an electron, the electric field pushes the electron out of the silicon junction. Metal conductive plates on the sides of the cell collect the electrons and transfer them to wires, allowing the electrons to flow like any other source of electricity.

Many cells linked together make up a solar panel.

First invented in 1954 at Bell Labs, solar cell technology is rapidly improving. As LiveScience.com reported in 2017, researchers have produced ultrathin, flexible solar cells that are only 1.3 microns thick—much less than the width of a human hair—and twenty times lighter than a sheet of office paper. Light, flexible solar cells such as these could be integrated into aerospace technology; wearable electronics, and architecture as rooftop shingles, roof tiles, and building facades.[63]

The amount of electricity a solar panel produces depends on three factors: the size of the panel, the efficiency of the solar cells inside, and the amount of sunlight the panel gets. Historically, most solar panels in a home or industrial installation have been about 5.5 feet tall and a little more than three feet wide, with 60 solar cells each. As of 2019, typical solar panel capacity averaged 360 watts of power. More efficient panels are more expensive and are usually only needed if the owner has limited space on their roof.[64]

---

[63] LiveScience.com. https://www.livescience.com/41995-how-do-solar-panels-work.html
[64] https://www.solarpowerrocks.com/solar-basics/how-much-electricity-does-a-solar-panel-produce/

Solar PV is now the sexiest, most on-trend renewable technology. Because of its dark, angular, geometric, and sophisticated aesthetic, there's an almost cult-like obsession with PV. The sun hits these panels and boom, just like magic electricity is created. Take this Minneapolis St. Paul Magazine picture of an IPS' solar installations proof that PV is en vogue:

Solar Hot Water Systems

Solar hot water is the ugly stepchild of solar energy. The technology has been around for a very long time. At its core, the process involves the heating of water using direct energy from sunlight. The concept comes from nature: shallow water near the shore is warmer compared to deeper water. This is because the shallow bottom reflects heat, trapping it in water.

Solar water heaters work by *collecting* heat from the sun and *trapping* it. The energy comes directly or via light-concentrating mirrors. In large-scale installations, mirrors may concentrate sunlight into a smaller collector.

Direct systems convert sunlight into energy for heating water through the use of a solar thermal collector, which either pumps the hot water ("active" systems, which need an external power source) or moves it by natural convection ("passive" systems, which need no other power source) into a hot water storage tank. Direct systems are typically used in warm climates where there is little likelihood of freezing temperatures.

Closed-loop, or indirect, systems use a non-freezing liquid (like the antifreeze in your car radiator) to collect heat from the sun and transfer it to water in a storage tank. The sun's thermal energy heats the fluid in the solar collectors. Then, this fluid passes through a heat exchanger in the storage tank, transferring heat to the water inside. The non-freezing fluid then cycles back to the collectors. These systems are often used in cold climates.

As of 2017, global solar hot water capacity is 472 GWth. The market is dominated by China, the United States, and Turkey. The leading countries by capacity per capita are Barbados, Austria, Cyprus, Israel, and Greece.[65]

In areas that receive a lot of sunlight hours per day solar thermal systems are a no-brainer. In Hawaii, solar thermal has been mandated for new construction homes. In California and Florida for instance you'll see quite a few thermal systems that heat swimming pools.

There have been relatively few innovations in this space because the systems are relatively simple - pumps, collectors, piping, and controls - that's about it. There hasn't been much room for improvement, and thus little corresponding investment in the technology.

---

[65] Ren21. https://www.ren21.net/reports/global-status-report/

Concentrating Solar Power (CSP)

CSP has been overtaken by the exponential improvements of PV, which is why little development has taken place since the early 2000s. Many people can picture CSP plants. They use mirrors and other methods to "concentrate" the sun's intensity to churn turbines to create electricity. Some of solar's most salient imagery is that of mirrors and towers in a desert, but these projects have become a thing of the past. But how do CSPs actually work?

In the United States, most industrial power plants have used non-renewable fossil fuels—coal, oil, or natural gas—to create tremendous amounts of heat, boil liquid, make steam, and turn large turbines connected to an electricity-producing generator.

Nuclear power plants also utilize this method. Most nuclear reactors are in Europe, North America, East Asia, and South Asia. The United States is the largest producer of nuclear power, while France has the largest share of electricity generated by nuclear power. But three serious nuclear power plant accidents—Three Mile Island in 1979, Chernobyl in 1986, and Fukushima in 2011—and many smaller incidents have spurred governments to curtail their construction and operation.

CSP's generate power using three technologies.

•**Tower systems** use a surrounding field of mirrors, called heliostats, to focus sunlight at the top of a tower, where there's a receiver containing salts. Salts become molten and flow into a traditional steam heat turbine. Molten salt efficiently retains heat, so it can be stored for days before being converted into electricity, allowing electricity to be produced several hours after sunset or on cloudy days.

The U.S. Department of Energy, along with several electric utilities, built and operated the first demonstration solar power tower near Barstow, California, during the 1980s and 1990s. Three solar power tower projects now operate in the United States, in Ivanpah Dry Lake in California, in Nevada, and in the Mojave Desert in Southern California.

• **Dish systems** use a mirrored dish to collect and concentrate the sun's heat onto a receiver, like the one used in a power tower system. To reduce costs, the mirrored dish is usually composed of many smaller flat mirrors formed into a dish shape.

•**Parabolic-trough** systems capture the sun's energy through long concave mirrors tilted toward the sun. At the center of each mirrored trough is a long pipe containing oil, which is heated and used to boil water in a conventional steam generator to produce electricity.

Parabolic trough linear concentrating systems are used in the longest operating solar thermal power facility in the world, the Solar Energy Generating System (SEGS). The facility, with nine separate plants, is located in the Mojave Desert in California.[66]

All three of these technologies use mechanical tracking systems that keep sunlight focused onto the receiver throughout the day as the sun changes position in the sky. They typically have a thermal energy storage system component that allows the solar collector system to release stored heat to produce electricity in the evening or during cloudy weather. They may also incorporate hybrid systems that use other fuels, typically natural gas, to supplement energy from the sun during periods of low solar radiation.

---

[66] https://www.eia.gov/energyexplained/solar/solar-thermal-power-plants.php

Wind

Humanity has been harnessing wind power for thousands of years. Wind-generated electricity began in the 1930s when Germany proposed building offshore wind turbines. It wasn't until 1991 when they were first installed in Sweden, and in Denmark the following year. By July 2010, there were 2.4 gigawatts of offshore wind turbines installed in Europe.

The principle is very simple: a big rotor mounted high on a pylon turns in the wind. It's connected directly to a generator, which creates electricity. A key component in the wind turbine is the efficiency and reliability of its drive train, which links the aerodynamic rotor and electrical output terminals. There are three main types of wind turbine generators (WTGs): direct current (DC), alternating current (AC) synchronous, and AC asynchronous generators. Each has its attributes and liabilities.

Wind turbines can be built in a wide range of sizes. Small turbines are used for applications such as battery charging for auxiliary power for boats or travel trailers (caravans in Europe) or to power traffic warning signs. The tiniest is the Blow Light, which features a 2.4-inch diameter rotor blade attached to a generator and small LED lights. You just hold it in your hand, blow on it, and it lights up![67]

Currently, the largest wind turbine is the Haliade-X 12 MW, which its maker, General Electric, claims is the most powerful offshore wind turbine in the world. It features a 12-megawatt capacity (the world's largest at the time of this writing), a 220-meter rotor, and a 107-meter blade. In addition to being the biggest offshore wind turbine, the Haliade-X will also be the most efficient wind turbine in the ocean.[68]

---

[67] https://inhabitat.com/worlds-smallest-wind-turbine/
[68] GE.com. https://www.ge.com/renewableenergy/wind-energy/offshore-wind/haliade-x-offshore-turbine

Large groups of turbines, known as wind farms, are becoming an increasingly important source of intermittent renewable energy. Despite the attraction of coal mining for local economies, China is betting heavily on onshore (inland) wind farms. For example, The Gansu Wind Farm Project or Jiuquan Wind Power Base is a group of large wind farms under construction in western Gansu province in China, with a planned capacity of 20 gigawatts. The project is one of six national wind power megaprojects approved by the Chinese government. The challenge for this installation—and many others in China—is that it's located along the Gobi Desert, where there are extremely high winds. But it's a thousand miles from China's highly populated port cities, and currently, there is a lack of infrastructure and transmission lines that would carry the power into the cities, where it's most needed.

In the United States, the biggest wind farm is the Alta Wind Energy Center, located in Tehachapi, Kern County, California. Also known as the Mojave Wind Farm, it has a combined installed capacity of about 1,550 megawatts.

Offshore, the United Kingdom is taking the lead. In June 2019, the first part of the world's largest and furthest-offshore wind farm came online at the Hornsea One wind farm. When its 174 turbines become fully operational in 2020, it will be capable of generating enough electricity to power a million homes. When completed, the project will have a generating capacity of 1.2 gigawatts, more than double the capacity of the current largest offshore wind installation, which also happens to be in the United Kingdom.

"Operating a wind farm this far offshore is unprecedented," David Coussens, the deputy operating manager for the wind farm, told the trade journal *Offshore Wind*. "We've had to think creatively and come up with new ways of working to overcome the logistical and technical challenges of operating a massive power station 120 kilometers from the shore."[69]

Geothermal

While the rocky, soil-covered surface of Earth is mainly stable and relatively inert, deep underground it's a different story. The amount of heat generated in Earth's interior—known as geothermal energy—is tremendous. The world's energy needs could be met many times over if we learned to effectively harness geothermal's power. The primary problem is that historically it's been very difficult to do so.

Today, geothermal energy is used in around 20 countries, with a total capacity of over 13GW installed worldwide by the end of 2018.[70] Plants that generate electricity use three types of geothermal energy. All three exploit the natural heat of the Earth, are non-polluting, and are indefinitely renewable. They use steam or hot water from reservoirs found several miles below the Earth's surface.

The three types of geothermal power plants are dry steam, flash steam, and binary cycle.

Dry steam power plants: These draw from naturally occurring underground resources of steam. The steam is piped directly from underground wells to the power plant, where it is directed into a turbine/generator unit.

In the United States, there are only two known underground resources of steam. One is Yellowstone National Park in Wyoming, which is the location of the famous geyser Old Faithful and is protected from development. The only dry steam plant in

---

[69] Gizmodo. https://earther.gizmodo.com/the-worlds-largest-offshore-wind-farm-just-came-online-1835215479
[70] https://www.power-technology.com/features/oldest-geothermal-plant-larderello/

the country is at The Geysers, located in the Mayacamas Mountains 72 miles (116 km) north of San Francisco, California. This happens to be the world's largest geothermal field, containing a complex of 22 geothermal power plants, drawing steam from more than 350 wells. It is estimated that the development meets 60 percent of the power demand for the coastal region between the Golden Gate Bridge and the Oregon state line.

Flash steam power plants: These are the most common. They use geothermal reservoirs of water with temperatures greater than 360°F (182°C). This very hot water flows up under its own pressure through production wells drilled into the ground. As it flows upward, the pressure decreases, and some of the hot water boils into steam. The steam is then separated from the water and used to power a turbine/generator. Leftover water and condensed steam are pumped back into the reservoir via injection wells, making this a sustainable resource.

The Larderello Geothermal Complex in Italy, first developed by Prince Piero Ginori Conti, now comprises 34 plants with a total net capacity of 769MW. The power generated by the complex accounts for approximately 10 percent of all geothermal energy produced worldwide and supplies 26.5 percent of regional power needs. It's also a tourist attraction, with Tuscany's geothermal areas receiving 120,000 visitors in 2017 alone. In fact, "geothermal tourism" is now an important part of the Tuscan geothermal district.

Binary cycle power plants: These operate using water at lower temperatures of about 225°-360°F (107°-182°C). They use the heat from the hot water to boil a working fluid, usually an organic compound with a low boiling point such as butane or pentane hydrocarbon. The working fluid is vaporized in a heat exchanger and used to turn a turbine. The cool water is then pumped back into the ground to be naturally reheated. The water from the geothermal reservoir never comes in contact with the turbine/generator units, and the water and working fluids are in separate systems. Binary cycle power plants are closed-loop systems, and only water vapor is emitted to the atmosphere.

Small-scale geothermal power plants: At under five megawatts, these have the potential for widespread application in rural areas, possibly even as distributed energy resources—that is, a variety of small, modular power-generating technologies that can be combined to improve the operation of the electricity delivery system.

As noted by the University of Twente at Geocap.nl, energy sources for small scale geothermal power plants can come from hot springs with adequate flow rate, wellhead generating units of high enthalpy (having a high heat content) wells, waste brine from high enthalpy power plants, low-medium enthalpy wellbores in a volcanic hydrothermal system, and low-medium enthalpy wellbores in a sedimentary basin system.[71]

Residential & Commercial Building Heat Pumps: Heat pumps are not geothermal in the same sense as geothermal power plants because they don't necessarily tap the vast reserves of underground heat in the Earth. They are devices that absorb heat from one medium (earth, water, or air) and transfer it to some other location, where it is released. Perhaps counterintuitively, heat pumps are used to transfer heat from a *lower* temperature source to one of a *higher* temperature. This is the

---

[71] https://www.geocap.nl/handbook/direct-use/small-scale-geothermal-power-plant/#contact

opposite of the natural flow of heat and is the same process that is used to extract heat in your home refrigerator.

(To transfer heat from a higher temperature area to a lower temperature area, you don't need a pump—the heat will flow on its own accord. Like when you open your oven door and the hot air comes pouring out into your cooler kitchen.)

Heat pumps do not generate heat and require an energy source only for the simple moving parts, which are the electric-powered pump or fan, and the compressor.

Geothermal heat pumps (GHPs): sometimes referred to as GeoExchange, earth-coupled, ground-source, or water-source heat pumps, have been in use since the late 1940s. This type of renewable energy depends not upon heat radiating from deep beneath the surface but on a different phenomenon—the fact that in the northern and southern latitudes, just below the surface the temperature of the soil remains constant. Although many parts of the globe experience seasonal temperature extremes, from blazing heat in the summer to freezing cold in the winter, depending on latitude, underground temperatures occupy a narrower range from 45°F (7°C) to 75°F (21°C). Like in a cave, during the winter the ground temperature tends to be warmer than the air above it, and in the summer it's cooler than the air. It stays the same from day into night, and throughout the change of seasons.

The idea is that if the subterranean earth was warmer than the air outside and, in your building, (that is, in wintertime), then you could transfer some of that heat energy into your building and make it warmer. Conversely, if it were a hot summer day and the earth was cooler, then you could capture some of that coolness to reduce the heat in your house.

For residential use, heat pumps can reduce energy use by 30 percent to 60 percent, control humidity, are sturdy and reliable, and fit in a wide variety of homes.

There are four basic types of geothermal heat pump systems for buildings. They are all "closed-loop" systems, which means they work like your home refrigerator or your car's radiator, by circulating a fluid that captures and then releases heat. These circulate an antifreeze solution through a closed-loop, usually made of plastic tubing, that is buried in the ground or submerged in water. A heat exchanger transfers heat between the refrigerant in the heat pump and the antifreeze solution in the closed-loop. Which one of these works best depends on the climate, soil conditions, available land, and local installation costs at the site.

Horizontal: This type requires a patch of available land in which trenches are dug at least four feet deep. The design can use either two pipes, with one buried at six feet, and the other at four feet, or two pipes placed side-by-side at five feet in the ground in a two-foot wide trench. During winter, the fluid in the pipes, which are placed below the frost line, is warmed by the earth. During summer, the fluid is cooled by the earth.

Vertical: Large commercial buildings with little surrounding land often use vertical systems, which go deep rather than wide. Holes, typically four inches in diameter, are drilled about 20 feet apart and 100 to 400 feet deep. Into these holes go two pipes that are connected at the bottom with a U-bend to form a loop.

Water source heat pump: If the site has an adequate water body, a supply line pipe is run underground from the building to the water and coiled into circles at least eight feet under the surface to prevent freezing.

Air source heat pump (ASHP): Also known as an air-to-air pump, this type extracts heat from outdoor air and transfers it into the home. Even relatively cold air actually contains a substantial amount of heat that can be collected. Under the principles of vapor compression refrigeration, an ASHP uses a refrigerant system involving a compressor and a condenser to absorb heat at one place and release it at another. This is one of the easiest and cheapest heat pumps to install and takes up little space.

Open-loop system: This uses renewable well or surface body water as the heat exchange fluid that circulates directly through the GHP system. This option is obviously practical only where there is an adequate supply of relatively clean water, and all local codes and regulations regarding groundwater discharge are met.

Hybrid heat pump: In areas with climates that range from hot in the summer to very cold in the winter, hybrid systems can boost efficiency. Ground and air source heat pump combinations use air-source systems when air is hot outside but switch to ground source when temperatures drop. Heat pump and gas/oil boiler combinations with simultaneous operation offer more consistent warmth at a higher level of efficiency. They are commonly used in homes with existing boiler systems.

Solar heat pump: All heat pump systems need some sort of electrically powered pump or fan, and often a compressor. Used in conjunction with air and geothermal heat pumps, solar heat pumps integrate solar panels as a power supply for the system. With a solar panel supplying electricity, it is, therefore, possible to heat and cool your home solely by renewable energy.

The geothermal energy sector is growing. Major factors driving the market include the global drive towards cleaner energy generation, supportive government policies, and increasing energy requirements across the planet.

Ocean Energy

Oceans cover more than 70 percent of the surface of the Earth, and according to the U.S. Geological Survey, they contain over 332 million cubic miles of water. These gigantic bodies of water are constantly in motion—from great ocean currents, to tides, to surface waves. Imagine capturing even a small amount of this hydrokinetic energy.

There are three basic types of ocean energy.

1. Waves

In many areas of the world, the wind blows with enough consistency and force to provide continuous waves along the shoreline. Harnessing this power has been a challenge. No commercial-scale wave power operations exist now, although a small-scale installation did operate off the coast of Portugal in 2008 and 2009. The Aguçadoura Wave Farm was a wave farm located 5 km (3 miles) offshore near Póvoa de Varzim north of Porto. The farm was designed to use three Pelamis Wave Energy Converters to convert the motion of the ocean surface waves into electricity. The long tube-like machines worked, but not well enough, and after a few months, they were shut down.

Wave power buoys capture the energy of the up-and-down movement of waves, generating power that is transmitted by an underwater cable to the electric grid onshore.

Most experts agree that wave power is where wind power was twenty years ago: the potential is obvious, but the technology hasn't yet been developed to exploit it. So far, the wave energy field comprises small companies working from small amounts of government funding when they can get it.

It's only a matter of time before someone figures it out. If you have engineering skills and an entrepreneurial spirit, maybe wave power is where you should focus your energy.

2. Tides

Tides are caused by the gravitational pull of the moon and sun along with the rotation of the earth. In some regions, tides cause water levels near the shore to vary up to forty feet, twice every day. Tide power is actually an ancient form; more than a thousand years ago, people in Europe harnessed the tidal flow of water to operate grain mills.

There are two basic approaches:

i. Barrage

This system uses a structure similar to a dam called a barrage, which utilizes turbines to capture the energy of moving water. Several tidal power barrages operate around the world. At 254 megawatts (MW), the largest electricity generation capacity is the Sihwa Lake Tidal Power Station in South Korea. The second-largest operating tidal power plant—which is also the oldest—is in La Rance, France, with 240 MW of electricity generation capacity.

ii. Seafloor turbine

The principle used by wind turbines can also be used in the ocean to capture tidal energy. Tidal turbines can be placed on the seafloor, near the shore, where there is strong tidal flow. There are definitely challenges; because water is about 800 times denser than air, the machines must be much sturdier and heavier than wind turbines. While tidal turbines are more expensive to build than wind turbines, they capture more energy with smaller blades.

Verdant Power, a prominent manufacturer and installer of tidal power and hydroelectric systems, has embarked on the Roosevelt Island Tidal Energy (RITE) Project, located on the East Channel of the East River. This is a tidal strait connecting Long Island Sound with the Atlantic Ocean in New York Harbor. On January 23, 2012, the Federal Energy Regulatory Commission (FERC) issued Verdant Power a ten-year license to install up to 1 MW of power (30 turbines/10 TriFrames) at the RITE Project, making it the first commercially-licensed tidal power project in the United States.[72]

3. Ocean Thermal Energy Conversion, or OTEC

This is a process that can produce electricity by using the temperature difference between deep cold ocean water and warm surface waters, particularly in tropical climates. The principle is the same as a heat exchanger. Warm seawater passes through an evaporator and vaporizes the working fluid, ammonia. The ammonia vapor passes through a turbine which turns a generator making electricity. The lower pressure vapor leaves the turbine and condenses in the condenser connected to a flow of deep cold seawater. The liquid ammonia leaves the condenser and is pumped to the evaporator to repeat the cycle.[73]

In 1974, the United States became involved in OTEC research with the establishment of the Natural Energy Laboratory of Hawaii Authority. One of the world's leading test facilities for OTEC technology, the laboratory operated a 250-kilowatt (kW) demonstration OTEC plant for six years in the 1990s. The United States Navy supported the development of a 105-kW demonstration OTEC plant at the laboratory site. In 2015, this

---

[72] https://www.verdantpower.com/riteproject
[73] https://www.makai.com/ocean-thermal-energy-conversion/

facility became operational and currently supplies electricity to the local electricity grid.[74]

Hydroelectric

This form needs no introduction—you are no doubt familiar with the big dams that exist all over the world, primarily to control floods and generate electricity. The first hydroelectric facility, a plant on the Fox River in Appleton, Wisconsin, began operations in 1882. Paper manufacturer H.F. Rogers was able to generate enough electricity to run the plant, a nearby building, and his own house.[75]

In my home state of Minnesota, the entire Minneapolis milling industry of the late 1800s was built by harnessing hydropower from the Mississippi River at St. Anthony Falls. That revolution gave rise to food giants like General Mills. In the 1900s Henry Ford utilized a small hydro project along the Mississippi near Fort Snelling in St. Paul for a sprawling auto manufacturing facility.

The largest hydroelectric power stations top the list of the largest power stations of any kind, they're also some of the largest artificial structures in the world. The biggest is the Three Gorges Dam, spanning the Yangtze River near Sandouping in Hubei province, China. Since 2012, the Three Gorges Dam has been the world's largest power station in terms of installed capacity (22,500 MW).

Clearly, while dams with hydroelectric capabilities have been a huge boost to our ability to generate power, many people don't consider them in the same class as true renewables because the number of dams that can be built is finite. There are only so many rivers in the world, and scientists have serious concerns about the impact these dams have on the environment. Although

---

[74] https://www.eia.gov/energyexplained/hydropower/ocean-thermal-energy-conversion.php
[75] https://www.nationalgeographic.org/thisday/sep30/first-hydroelectric-plant-opens/

hydroelectric power does not pollute the air, it disrupts waterways and freshwater ecosystems and disturbs the animals that live in them, changing currents, water levels, and migration paths for many aquatic species.

Biomass

Biomass is organic matter that comes from recently living plants and organisms. It's the most ancient form of energy used by humans since we first began burning wood to cook our food and keep warm. Especially in developing nations, wood is still the largest biomass energy resource today. In 2017, energy from biomass made up about five percent of the total energy used in the United States. This energy came from wood, biofuels like ethanol, and energy generated from methane captured from landfills or by burning municipal waste.[76]

The most common biomass materials used for energy are plants like corn and soy. Biomass can be used for fuels, power production, and petroleum-based products such as plastics that would otherwise be made from fossil fuels.

Many renewable energy experts are unenthusiastic about biomass energy. The challenge of biomass energy is that the source, such as corn, needs to be grown; and then to release energy it needs to be processed and burned. Not much different from petroleum products. In addition, competition for arable lands required for food and fiber production is a major issue. Biomass feedstock production and utilization of agricultural and forest residues for energy can lead to nutrient depletion, soil disturbance, and reduced water quality.

For the reasons above, biomass' future is likely limited as electrification of transportation will be swift and all-

---

[76] https://www.justenergy.com/blog/7-types-of-renewable-energy-the-future-of-energy/

encompassing. At the very least it's worth including here for context, as it will still have some application during the transitionary period between now and then.

Energy Storage

A critical step toward further renewable energy integration will be the advent of energy storage technology. Wind and solar energy, intermittent resources, need applications to help them disburse power when the skies are calm or dark. There are many emerging technologies to fill this void, including lithium-ion, flow batteries, pumped hydro, and future technology like graphene and zinc-air.

Lithium-Ion

This is probably the most well-known battery option. The majority of new home energy storage technologies use some form of lithium-ion. It's become the standard for two reasons.

1) It's much more compact than heavy lead-acid batteries - requiring the least amount of space & labor.

2) Lithium-Ion batteries have a longer lifespan than almost all comparable batteries - including lead-acid batteries.

The only downside to Lithium-Ion batteries has been higher costs per unit. Given the extended lifespan and design benefits many are still willing to utilize them over alternative options.

On the side of solar energy storage, experts agree Lithium-Ion batteries have been the ideal option due to their "relatively high energy density (up to 200 Wh/kg), high EE (more than 95%), and long cycle life (3000 cycles at deep discharge of 80%). Thus far,

77% of electrical power storage systems in the USA that operate to stabilize the grid (e.g., primarily for regulating frequency) rely on LIBs, indicating a high-value market for LIBs."-

However, many solar experts express a differing opinion in which they feel alternative battery options should be further developed for energy storage. Beyond cost-control issues, lithium-ion cells and batteries do not have robust technology and usage-protection as other rechargeable batteries meaning they must be monitored for overcharge and discharge. Aging is another disadvantage of LIBS. These batteries will only be able to withstand 500, 100 percent charge-discharge cycles, on average, before their capacity is significantly impacted.[77]

Flow

Flow batteries are an alternative energy storage option. They are systems of two connected tanks of electrolyte liquids. One tank holds positively charged cathode while the other holds negatively charged anode. The electricity flows between the tanks via a membrane connecting them.

According to research from Irina Slav, a journalist focusing on technology in the oil and gas industry, "flow batteries have longer lives because the electric current flowing from tank to tank does not degrade the membrane. True flow batteries are also called redox flow batteries, after the two reactions they utilize: reduction, or a gain of electrons, and oxidation, or loss of electrons from electrolyte liquid to electrolyte liquid."[78]

---

[77] https://www.electronics-notes.com/articles/electronic_components/battery-technology/li-ion-lithium-ion-advantages-disadvantages.php
[78] https://oilprice.com/Alternative-Energy/Renewable-Energy/Are-Flow-Batteries-The-Future-Of-Energy-Storage.html

Pumped Hydro

Pumped storage hydropower is classified as a hydroelectric energy storage source. Essentially, power is generated by connecting two water sources at different elevations. As the water moves down through a turbine between the water sources, it draws power from pumping water from the water source at a higher elevation.

According to research from the Energy Storage Association, "Pumped storage stations are unlike traditional hydroelectric stations in that they are a net consumer of electricity, due to hydraulic and electrical losses incurred in the cycle of pumping from lower to upper reservoirs. However, these plants are typically highly efficient (round-trip efficiencies reaching greater than 80%), and can prove very beneficial in terms of balancing load within the overall power system. Pumped-storage facilities can be very economical due to peak and off-peak price differentials and their potential to provide critical ancillary grid services."[79]

Graphene

One of the more promising energy storage technologies on the horizon is Graphene, which is a 2D material composed of all carbon atoms arranged in a hexagonal lattice. Most forms of graphene allow for high electrical conductivity. They've been shown to exhibit great charge carrier mobility, as well as high stability making it an ideal candidate for renewable energy storage.

Graphene-based batteries have been extensively tested in academic laboratories. However, they are now entering the commercialization stage. These batteries are being produced by

---

[79] https://energystorage.org/why-energy-storage/technologies/pumped-hydropower/

some of the largest names in the energy industry including Samsung.

Zinc Air

Zinc-air batteries work by utilizing available oxygen from the air to extract power from zinc. Because zinc is one of the most abundant elements on earth, the production costs for this form of energy storage battery can be very low. As an additional benefit, these batteries are proven to be safer and more resilient than lithium-ion, flow, and lead-acid batteries.

The primary disadvantage of zinc-air batteries stem from the recharging process. Design Labs explains the complexities of the reverse charge process. Reversing this process to recharge the battery has proved difficult for scientists. Like lithium and many other metals, zinc batteries can suffer from unstable charging. A company called EnZinc has developed a unique battery, utilizing technology originally created by the U.S. Naval Research Laboratory. The company claims it can increase stability with novel anode and cathode designs. Zinc-air is one of a handful of promising technologies that could revolutionize energy and transportation. Winners will emerge over the next decade and shape the future in ways that today seem impossible.

Energy Efficiency

Energy efficiency is by far the most diverse energy market in clean energy, encompassing everything from efficient appliances to light bulbs to weatherization. It's low hanging fruit; after all, the cheapest kilowatt hour is the one you never use. For all its practicality, efficiency is consistently picked on as clean energy's most boring segment, but it certainly has the biggest impact per dollar spent.

The first real efficiency initiative was the energy conservation movement between 1973 and 1981. While well-intended, its influence was muted. Much of the program's emphasis was centered on the necessity to "save" energy. Advertising was primarily comprised of "switch it off" messaging.

In the early 1980s, the approach to energy efficiency focused on energy management. With new technology, large businesses and municipalities began monitoring their energy usage and they even hired experts in the field to manage it. These initiatives were fairly exclusive to large corporations and did not include individuals, small businesses and rural communities.

Due in part to the success of the 1980's campaigns utilities began selling energy at extremely low rates. As a response, large corporations began reversing their previous conservation efforts. Dr. Steven Fawkes explained, "as energy prices declined in real terms, and opportunities for effective purchasing strategies were opened up by market liberalization, most of the attention on energy shifted purely to purchasing. Greater savings with less risk could be made through more effective purchasing rather than implementing energy efficiency projects. Many energy managers were made redundant or transferred into other jobs and many large organizations which had been pioneers of energy management started to lose ground."

As climate change and environmental concerns gained momentum in the mid 2000s, energy efficiency evolved again. Still largely excluding individuals and rural entities, large corporations and municipalities began to prioritize carbon reduction. Largely supported by state governments, many utilities decoupled energy generation from energy profits. This meant that utilities could maintain profits even if they produced and sold less energy. Overnight these actions motivated utilities to create massive efficiency campaigns, implementing rebate programs for new lightbulbs and appliances.

The current evolution of energy control is modern energy efficiency as we know it today. Smart devices that can modulate power consumption and AI technology that learns and becomes more efficient over time. Data is now king in the space and opening up new opportunities never thought possible just a decade ago. Accommodating the deluge of renewable resources will require consumption on the grid to become even smarter; efficiency will be a major factor in driving the clean energy future forward.

Cleantech's Future with Jake Rozmaryn

As head of publicity powerhouse Antenna Group, Jake Rozmaryn is responsible for the agency's work in clean energy, smart mobility, sustainable tech, environmental impact, and emerging technologies.

Jake founded Eco Branding in 2011, which was successfully acquired by Antenna in 2017. He's helped launch dozens of cleantech, mobility, and sustainability startups, previously served as CEO & Founder of Eco Branding, and was recognized as a Forbes 30 Under 30 in Energy in 2018. Needless to say, his exposure to many different industry trends makes him uniquely qualified to comment on the future of energy.

When asked to predict the trends that will most impact the space over the next decade he responded:

There have been these dominant modalities in cleantech – clean energy, electric vehicles, energy efficiency – but it's expanded exponentially over recent years. I used to think about cleantech as this defined thing but today I look at every sector in the economy and ask "where can we find cleantech disruption?" Innovation in any sector about creating better systems, utilizing waste, and finding efficiencies. You can find cleantech in everything, it's just about being smart and identifying opportunities.

*When I look at areas today that are going to be the next big mega trends, I think about **carbon technologies**. I think about carbon capture, utilization, sequestration, and direct air capture. Extracting carbon from industrial waste to repurpose it for some kind of second life. There are companies today refining captured carbon into concrete; that solution will only improve over time.*

*The **agriculture** space broadly is ripe for disruption. Whether it relates to innovations in indoor ag, artificial intelligence (AI), internet of things (IOT), vertical farming, drip irrigation, food surveying to optimize how fields are being tilled. The largest disruption in food is the rise of plant-based proteins – things like Impossible Foods and Beyond Meat. In a little more than a year 5% of Burger King sales are coming from the Impossible Whopper, a meatless hamburger. Now they're rolling out three more plant-based protein options. Think about the potential for exponential growth; it could change livestock and how we think about animals.[80]*

*The **Circular Economy** has become a big umbrella term. There's more emphasis on circular supply chains, like the end of fast*

---

[80] As mentioned earlier, nearly 25% of global GHG emissions are related to methane produced by the factory farming of livestock.

fashion in favor of sustainable fashion. Across industries like automotive, agriculture, furniture, and more – we need solutions because business-as-usual is untenable.

Connectivity *is exciting. Systems are starting to work together; the integration of solar and batteries, electric vehicles, and the grid, home automation, and intelligent connected devices will have a material impact on communities in significant ways. Connectivity will accelerate with the advent of smarter AI, faster 5G, and the integration of more connected devices. The synchronization of these things will allow technology to work smarter, harder, and better for people.*

I've been very excited to see that every company, every brand, and organization, whatever they do, they understand the situation today why all of this stuff is important, inter-divesting from oil and gas making huge investments in renewables and grid modernization, consumer giants are looking for more ways to become more sustainable, real estate developers are thinking about how to decarbonize their buildings. These things did not exist 10 years ago.

Things are starting to happen at a much more exponential pace because companies and cities are motivated. People want to live in cities that are cleaner, work for companies that are more sustainable, and eat at restaurants that have more sustainable options. There's a convergence of things happening in the world that accelerate the pace of adoption and awareness.

5. Clean Energy Career Opportunities

After an overview of the clean energy industry, your next question likely is, "What kind of career opportunities are there, and what qualifications do I need to be successful?"

In this chapter, we'll review careers that can be considered unique or special to core activities of the clean energy sector. Much like any industry clean energy companies employ marketing people and accountants and human resource managers, these are equivalent positions for which special training or education in renewable energy is probably not necessary.

Clean energy jobs were growing rapidly heading into the COVID19 slowdown, and is likely to rebound quickly. According to the U.S. Department of Energy, 6.4 million Americans now work in the Traditional Energy and Energy Efficiency industries, which added over 300,000 net new jobs in 2016, accounting for 14 percent of the nation's job growth. Energy efficiency jobs increased by 133,000, for a total of 2.2 million. Investments in energy transmission, distribution, and storage (our energy infrastructure) generated 65,000 new jobs.

Solar industry employment jumped by over 73,000 jobs or 25 percent, while wind industry employment added 25,000 new jobs for a total of 102,000.[81]

Energy.gov provides a report on the fastest-growing career opportunities in clean energy. Here are some of them:

Wind Technician

A wind turbine technician, also known as a "windtech," installs, inspects, maintains, operates, and repairs wind turbines. They are able to diagnose and fix any problem that could cause the turbine to fail. They service underground transmission systems, wind field substations, and fiber optic sensing and control systems. They collect turbine data for testing or research and analysis.

To do their work, windtechs use a variety of hand and power tools, as well as computers to diagnose electrical or software malfunctions. Wind turbines integrate most monitoring equipment into the nacelle, which can be viewed on site. And yes, if you want to be a windtech, you need to be willing to climb to the top of a 200-foot tower. When repairing blades, windtechs rappel from the turbine's hub to the section of the blade that needs servicing. This might be harrowing for those of you with an aversion to heights, but the views are amazing!

Wind turbine technician isn't just *one* of the fastest-growing jobs in clean energy, it's the *single fastest*-growing occupation in America. According to the Bureau of Labor Statistics, employment

---

[81] US DOE. https://www.energy.gov/articles/doe-releases-second-annual-national-energy-employment-analysis-0

in the sector will grow by 108 percent by 2024. The median annual wage of a windtech is $52,260.

Clean Energy Project Developer

Clean energy project developers[82] are one of the fast-growing roles in the industry. This job requires candidates to have a mastery of project management skills. While the position greatly varies based on what corporation or company you work for, the major function of the position is to effectively manage solar power plant projects. In order to succeed in a clean energy project developer role, you must properly evaluate risk, anticipate and prepare mitigation plans, and manage pre-construction operations.

Another major focus of clean energy development is managing cash flow and the project timeline. There are a lot of moving parts associated with these aspects of wind and solar projects. Clean energy project developers need to successfully manage contracts to optimize supply costs. Effective scheduling is incredibly important. If a project falls behind schedule, it could mean increased labor costs and a backlog of other services that can no longer be implemented as planned.

While the role is definitely challenging, it has a lot of rewarding attributes too. Starting in a clean energy project developer role gives new entrees to the industry a full-spectrum view of the time and resources needed to complete renewable development projects. With this experience, the options for future career growth are versitle. Additionally, salaries tend to scale quite a bit depending on the size of the organization and the quantity and magnitude of the projects. While starting salaries average around $45,000, positions can range to salaries averaging

---

[82] I'd worn this hat at IPS for a handful of years.

around $130,000. Additional commissions and bonuses are also commonplace.

Green Building Professional

Buildings constructed today are inherently very different from those built a century ago. As support for protecting the environment grows, "green" or sustainable buildings have become more commonplace. Green construction is the practice of erecting or remodeling buildings to be resource-efficient and environmentally responsible. While these buildings might not look much different from their predecessors, they feature specialized designs and materials to limit their energy consumption and environmental impact.

Creating green buildings requires skilled workers, including architects, construction managers, and carpenters, with knowledge of new design and training in construction techniques. Many organizations, both local and national, offer training for green construction trades. The National Center for Construction Education and Research (NCCER), a non-profit foundation dedicated to developing standardized construction training programs, has created several green training modules recognized by the U.S. Green Building Council (USGBC) and Green Building Certification Institute.[83]

The most popular certification for sustainable construction is Leadership in Energy and Environmental Design (LEED) which is curated by the USGBC. New construction or existing buildings can be certified as meeting certain green thresholds, which qualifies those properties for different levels of sustainable bling. Many architects, engineers, and urban planners who work in green

---

[83] https://www.bls.gov/green/construction/

construction have the LEED Accredited Professional (AP) credential.

Building more environmentally sustainable buildings and houses requires expertise across a range of professionals in design and construction, from architects and engineers to carpenters and heavy equipment operators.

Overall, nearly 1.4 million energy efficiency jobs are in the construction industry. Construction firms have seen a significant increase in the percentage of their workforce that spends at least half their time on work related to improving energy efficiency, rising from approximately 65 percent in 2015 to 74 percent in 2016.

Engineers, architects, and urban planners working in green building design need to have at least a bachelor's degree in a relevant discipline, and many jobs require more education, such as a master's degree or professional degree.

Solar Installer

The vast majority of solar panel installation work is done outdoors, but it sometimes require work in attics and other interior spaces to interconnect with a building's electrical infrastructure. Much is done manually, installing panels on metal racks and configuring that racking on the roof or ground.

Installers must travel to various job sites throughout the year. For larger ground-mounted projects that typically requires being away from home, mostly in rural areas, for weeks or months at a time. Residential and commercial installers work on roofs closer to urban areas and are less likely to travel long distances. Seasonality may also come into play with most installation activity in North America happening outside of winter, usually from March through December.

According to recruiter.com, the current median wage is $48,700 per year in the US, but jobs in certain states like New York can pay considerably more ($71,030). The educational qualification is a high school diploma, but being a licensed electrician is a big asset if you want to move up to higher pay.

Overall, the solar industry added more than 73,000 jobs in 2016—a 25 percent increase over 2015. It's estimated that one out of every fifty new jobs created nationally came from solar. The core growth opportunity in this space continues to be solar installers.

Employment of solar PV installers is projected to grow 63 percent from 2018 to 2028, much faster than the average for all occupations. Continued expansion and adoption of solar will result in excellent long-term opportunities for qualified individuals, particularly those who complete photovoltaic courses at technical schools or private training facilities.[84]

Sustainability Specialist

In addition to designing and building new homes and facilities, there are an increasing number of career opportunities focused on making our existing buildings more energy-efficient, sustainable, and resilient. A growing network of experts, consultants, and energy managers are responsible for creating and implementing plans to meet these goals and champion greater efficiencies in their facilities. Due to their potential for considerable cost savings and a vital link between organization and regulation, sustainability specialists are now a vital part of many organizations. Their role is largely a practical one: To develop methods of fostering sustainability at all levels of the business, creating better processes to conserve resources.

---

[84] US BLS. https://www.bls.gov/ooh/construction-and-extraction/solar-photovoltaic-installers.htm

At colleges and universities, there are a growing number of degree programs that help qualify you for a career as a Sustainability Specialist. They include master of public administration (MPA) in environmental science and policy, master of arts in climate and society, Ph.D. in sustainable development, an undergraduate major in sustainable development, MPA in development practice, master of science in sustainability management, and master of science in sustainability science.

Through its Better Buildings Initiative, the U.S. Department of Energy has helped establish national guidelines for professional certification programs. This can improve the quality of workforce credentials for energy auditors, managers, and other efficiency-related occupations.

According to PayScale in December 2017, the average salary for a sustainability specialist in the USA is $53,842. The typical range is $41,107 for those at the lowest end of the pay scale up to $77,455 for those at the highest end of the pay scale.[85]

Clean Car Engineer

The automotive industry employs thousands of mechanical, electrical, and software engineers to design and manufacture new vehicles. A subset of this vast pool of engineers are those who specialize in alternative fuel and all-electric vehicles. As more and more alternative fuel vehicles hit the streets, opportunities are growing related to sustainable transportation. Today more than 259,000 Americans work with these vehicles, including cars and trucks running on electricity, hydrogen, and other alternative fuels.[86] These jobs primarily fall within various disciplines of engineering, like chemical, materials, electrical, and mechanical.

---

[85] https://www.environmentalscience.org/career/sustainability-specialist
[86] https://www.energy.gov/eere/articles/5-fastest-growing-jobs-clean-energy

Careers in the fuel efficiency component parts space represent almost 500,000 estimated U.S. jobs.

As James Ayre in *CleanTechnica* reported, the world's top auto manufacturers have pledged over $90 billion in capital for the development of electric vehicles and associated battery tech. For example, Ford Motor Company recently announced that it's investing $11 billion into EV development. Much of that outlay will be for more engineers. The plug-in electric vehicle sector currently represents less than one percent of the total global auto market, and that percentage is destined to grow significantly behind national priorities from countries like China. Most major auto manufacturers predict substantial market growth for EV's over the next decade and beyond.[87]

These are just a microcosm of the many career options available in clean energy. The following chapters will cover how to position yourself for success in the most dynamic market on the planet.

---

[87]https://www.powerelectronics.com/markets/automotive/article/21864240/the-ev-revolution-will-require-more-engineers

Career Advice from Jigar Shah

Arguably no one has shaped the future of solar more than Jigar Shah. As a founder of SunEdison he helped to revolutionize consumer adoption of clean energy by creating *Solar as a Service*. He's also the co-host of Energy Gang, an influential  industry podcast. In 2013 I had the good fortune of meeting Jigar on his book tour in support of *Creating Climate Wealth*, a book that helped to transform my thinking about solar and the future.

What are some common themes or personal characteristics shared by successful clean energy leaders?

Energy leaders are a bit different than most entrepreneurs as most have to deal with incumbents, policy, and finance. The most successful leaders realize that all three are important and that no one person has a mastery over any of them. Putting together teams with very different skill are critical to success.

You're often referred to as the Godfather of the Power Purchase Agreement, what are one or two of your lesser-known professional achievements that you'd wish more people knew about?

My biggest achievement has been the alumni of SunEdison. Many have gone on to prominent roles in the energy and decarbonization sectors. In fact, collectively they continue to do more good than I will ever do in my lifetime. The other accomplishment is to make our industry one that is accessible to all who wish to join. Through my various social media accounts, the Energy Gang podcast, and other media I work hard to demystify our space so that others can join us and call our industry their home.

If you can share, do you have any singular moments that you'd approach differently related to SunEd?

I never carry regrets. I make the best decisions I can at the time that I make them. Certainly, in hindsight, Goldman Sachs turned out to be a terrific tax equity partner and a terrible corporate equity partner. We had other prominent investors competing to invest into SunEdison and all of them would have been better than Goldman.

Generate Capital focuses on a variety of different cleantech solutions. What opportunities are you most excited about in the next five years? Why?

I work hard to be universally excited by all climate solutions and not anyone in particular. Climate solutions rarely succeed because they are supposed to. They succeed because they feature good teams, a well-understood product/market fit, and have a policy that is accommodating. I am always looking for that formula and when I find it I get excited.

On the Energy Gang, you're known as an extreme realist, which I (and many others) definitely appreciate. What somewhat controversial viewpoints might you hold in contrast to most other clean energy leaders?

I am not loved for my appreciation of fracking. I also don't think people are happy for my continued advocacy of phasing down solar and wind tax credits.

If you could give one piece of advice to someone exploring career opportunities in clean energy, what would it be?

Take whatever decent job offer comes your way. Even if that is in the oil and gas industry. You don't have to stay there forever and the experience is very valuable as you move around the industry to end up at your final goal.

Anything else you'd like to address?

We are lucky to be able to be part of this moment. This is our way to give back and help society while earning a solid living. I am forever grateful for the positive impact I am able to have in people's lives.

Defining What's Important

Everyone has a unique story or pathway as to how they arrived at the present. From a young age, I had typical interests—science, math, sports, music—but few passions. Often you hear of some *wunderkind* who obsessed over a hobby or skill and developed into virtuosic talent, reaching the highest echelons of their field before they could even get a driver's license. That wasn't me. I backed into business school as an alternative to the early morning class schedule of an engineering degree. When you think about it, choosing a career based on teenage sleep habits was not smart, but it worked out.

Speaking of not smart, I had the privilege of earning university credits by taking community college courses in high school. I came to college with a full semester under my belt, along with two full-ride scholarships and another partial scholarship. I was essentially getting paid to go to college, and with that honor do you think I chose to buckle down and get the most out of my education?

Nope. I chose to waste most of my time drinking beer and screwing around. Instead of graduating in four or maybe even three years, I took a healthy five and a half years to graduate. I have few regrets, but a big one that young people should consider is that there's a false dichotomy between applying oneself in college and having fun. You absolutely can do both!

In the mid-2000s, I tried to be a rock star, like the second coming of Prince[88]. I was totally into it. In college, I cared about few things more than picking up a guitar, making songs, and the idea of being chased by legions of adoring fans. But I slowly realized that my music was just marginally better than mediocre.

---

[88] Even though he was still alive at the time, and I had about 5% of his talent. In Minneapolis, as you can imagine, Prince is ubiquitous.

As the years wore on, I realized that what mattered most to me at age twenty didn't mean as much at twenty-five.

In 2006, just after my super-senior year in college, I was spending a ton of time just aimlessly apathetic, seeing my friends with their new Fortune 500 jobs. They had life figured out. Nothing really inspired me then. I suppose most everyone feels similarly at one point or another, and many spend years or decades in that limbo. We can all get bogged down in the slog of day-to-day life, and it can be difficult to step back and assess what's truly important. Luckily for me, that search came at a time with few real-life responsibilities. Many have challenges far greater than mine were, and to those people: a thousand well wishes on your journeys.

That same year, the documentary *An Inconvenient Truth* was released to mild fanfare and an Oscar. I rented the DVD and was immediately floored. As outlined in Chapter 1, anyone who sees the correlation between CO_2 and global temperature over time can appreciate the urgency needed to keep this world from catching fire and destroying humanity's future.

Having little more than a business degree and moderate drive for success, I sent resumes out to dozens of companies. Innovative Power Systems was the only one to respond, and the rest as they say is history. I'll continue to dig into my professional story in subsequent chapters, but now that you understand the technologies and some of the career options available to prospective job-seekers let's review the grittier details of cleantech.

6. Growing Pains

"I've had many failures in terms of technological... business... and even research failures. I really believe that entrepreneurship is about being able to face failure, manage failure, and succeed after failing."

- Kiran Mazumdar-Shaw, Indian billionaire entrepreneur.

"In the business world today, failure is apparently not an option. We need to change this attitude toward failure - and celebrate the idea that only by falling on our collective business faces do we learn enough to succeed down the road."

- Naveen Jain, business executive, entrepreneur, and the founder and former CEO of InfoSpace.

"Failure is not the opposite of success; it's part of success."

- Arianna Huffington, author, publisher, syndicated columnist, and businesswoman.

It hasn't been an easy road for clean energy. Like many industries, its history is spotted with ups and downs. But in many ways' failure is required for progress.

When Martin Luther King Jr. marched in Selma, Alabama, he and his supporters risked their lives against powerful opposition.

When Neil Armstrong and Buzz Aldrin stepped onto the Moon for the very first time, their journey was a culmination great risk by other astronauts and scientists, years in the making.

Embracing risk in the pursuit of progress can be costly, and many pay the ultimate sacrifice. When Christa McAuliffe and the other six crew members of the space shuttle Challenger ascended from the launch pad at Cape Kennedy on January 28, 1986, they knew they were taking a risk—and sadly, their mission ended in tragedy.

Nothing in this world of substance was created without risk; success and failure are its natural consequences. Blind exuberance and hubris play a part in failure as well. The Great Recession for instance was significantly predicated on speculative lending in the housing sector, where companies (and borrowers) took on too much risk and failed dramatically. These conditions led directly to the disintegration of Lehman Brothers and other American business pillars. Anyone who invests in a company is taking on risk, and companies in all industries regularly go bankrupt, with great financial losses to their investors.

New products can tank as well—sometimes spectacularly. In 1960, the failure of the Edsel, Ford Motor Company's "car of the future," cost Ford $250 million from the car's development, manufacturing, and marketing. It was such a disaster that the very name "Edsel" quickly became a popular label for product failure. And yet fifty years later, the Ford Motor Company is going strong. It's the sixth-largest auto manufacturer in the world and still one of the most iconic brands.

Apple—which has been ranked as the most valuable company in the world—has had its share of massive product missteps. In 2014, someone at Apple had the idea to team up with rock band U2 and give the group's new LP, "Songs of Innocence," to every one of the company's 500 million iTunes users. But the album wasn't just *offered* for free, it was shoved into every users' library without consent. Users felt violated,[89] music retailers felt cheated

---

[89] Along with their ears.

for being cut out of the U2 profit parade, and other musicians were rightfully enraged because the campaign promoted messaging that music should be free.[90]

More than six years later, both Apple and U2 seemed to have done okay after debacle, although some would argue that the band lost "street cred."[91]

Processes can fail, with costly results. On March 24, 1989, the oil tanker *Exxon Valdez* struck the Bligh Reef in Prince William Sound, near Tatitlek, Alaska. Over the next few days, the crippled ship leaked 10.8 million US gallons of crude oil. It's considered to be one of the worst human-caused environmental disasters in US waters, second only to the 2010 *Deepwater Horizon* oil spill. The remote location of Prince William Sound—it's accessible only by helicopter, plane, or boat—made industry and government response efforts very difficult. The region is a rich habitat for salmon, sea otters, seals, and seabirds, and thousands were either killed or had to be cleaned by hand. The oil eventually affected 1,300 miles of coastline, of which 200 miles were heavily or moderately oiled.

In 2014—twenty-five years later—the effects of the oil spill were still present. Federal scientists estimated that as much as 21,000 US gallons of oil remained on beaches in Prince William Sound and in locations up to 450 miles away. *Even after twenty-five years,* much of the oil did not appear to have biodegraded. A USGS scientist who analyzed the remaining oil along the coastline stated that it remained lodged among rocks, between tide marks. "The oil mixes with seawater and forms an emulsion...Left out, the surface crusts over but the inside still has the consistency of mayonnaise or mousse."[92]

---

[90] In reality, Apple paid U2 and its record company as much as $100 million.
[91] Arguably that was lost a while back – anyone remember the Batman Forever soundtrack?
[92] Walters, Joanna (March 23, 2014). "Exxon Valdez – 25 years after the Alaska oil spill, the court battle continues".

According to CBS, Exxon spent more than $3.8 billion in clean-up costs, fines, and compensation. Today, the ExxonMobil Corporation remains one of the world's largest companies by revenue, earning $279.3 billion in 2018, and has varied from the first to sixth-largest publicly traded company by market capitalization.

Companies of all types rise and fall, stumble and get up again, soar, and then crash. This is capitalism, and the concept of "survival of the fittest" is part of what makes our free market system so powerful.

Capitalism is also the source of many ecological issues we are faced with today. Our voracious appetite for quarterly growth, GDP, and resources are crowding out the needs of our planet. Take plastic bottles for instance – in a 2017 article, the Guardian newspaper[93] examined this issue and found that more than 1,000,000 plastic bottles are sold *every minute*; a figure that's projected to rise 20% by 2021. "Between 5,000,000 and 13,000,000 *tons* of plastic leaks into the world's oceans each year to be ingested by sea birds, fish, and other organisms, and by 2050 the ocean will contain more plastic by weight than fish, according to research by the Ellen MacArthur Foundation."[94] These bottles and other plastic waste are creating massive floating islands like the Great Pacific garbage patch,[95] which boasts an estimated 80,000 metric tons of plastic, totaling 1.8 trillion pieces that have coalesced across 1.6 million square kilometers.

Consumerism requires enormous amounts of resources to process and transport goods. In order for capitalism to work for everyone, including Earth, it absolutely must take into account lifecycle costs, including CO2 and other forms of pollution, which

---

[93] https://www.theguardian.com/environment/2017/jun/28/a-million-a-minute-worlds-plastic-bottle-binge-as-dangerous-as-climate-change
[94] https://www.ellenmacarthurfoundation.org/assets/downloads/EllenMacArthurFoundation_TheNewPlasticsEconomy_15-3-16.pdf
[95] https://en.wikipedia.org/wiki/Great_Pacific_garbage_patch

corporations are exploiting mostly at no cost, and mostly to the public's detriment.

As emerging technologies, clean energy has seen its share of successes and failures. The latter is perfectly normal and shouldn't surprise anyone.

I bring this up because it's fair to examine both sides of any argument.

The history of renewables is important for you to know for this reason: if you become a part of an industry, and you're involved in selling its services or equipment, or you're looking for investors, you'll quickly learn that many people know these gnawing anecdotes and some will point to them as reasons for opposition. Reciting the failures of companies in the clean energy sector is a favorite pastime of opponents. By being well equipped to counter their arguments, you'll be in a better position to win converts.

And make no mistake: the fossil fuel industry has powerful allies in government. Certain administrations like that of President Trump proudly and publicly align themselves with the coal, oil, and natural gas industries. Trump's efforts to prop up the fossil fuel industry by slashing regulations began with the precipitous withdrawal from the landmark 2015 Paris climate change accord, which 195 countries signed to help reduce rising global temperatures. He ended the Obama administration's Clean Power Plan rules to curb coal-fired power plant emissions and curtailed an Obama-era regulation designed to reduce methane emissions, which scientists regard as an even more dangerous greenhouse gas than carbon dioxide.

His administration also tapped two former energy lobbyists to run key departments—David Bernhardt as Secretary of the Interior and Andrew Wheeler, who was a coal lobbyist, as head of the Environmental Protection Agency. The EPA senior attorney,

Erik Baptist, is a former lobbyist and lawyer for the American Petroleum Institute.

Talking points from the anti-renewable crowd include:

- Noise from wind turbines may cause cancer.
- Wind turbines cause property values to plummet.
- If wind powers our electricity, your TV set will go off when the wind stops blowing.

In order to understand where the detractors are coming from and counter their arguments it's helpful to review some growing pains felt on behalf of the renewables industry. These are stories of mixed success and sometimes outright failure, which your skeptical investor or underwriter may cite as objections.

Solyndra, TenK & Standardization

Even today—nine years after it folded—clean energy opponents malign the government's investment in Solyndra. Based in Fremont, California the company that designed, manufactured, and sold unique, integrated solar PV system. The panels and mounting hardware were designed for large, low-slope commercial rooftops and had an unmistakable look.

Unlike today's familiar flat panels, the company's product used racks of cylindrical tubes, also called tubular solar panels, made of copper indium gallium selenite (CIGS). The company claimed this was a superior technology that, because of the curved surface of the tubes, would capture solar energy evenly throughout the day.

Under President Barack Obama's economic stimulus program, the American Recovery and Reinvestment Act of 2009, Solyndra received a $535 million U.S. Department of Energy loan guarantee. Additionally, the company received a $25.1 million tax break from California's Alternative Energy and Advanced Transportation Financing Authority. Unfortunately, it was later revealed that Solyndra officials used inaccurate information to mislead the Department of Energy in its application.

Another, smaller example was TenKsolar, a boutique solar manufacturer based in Minnesota. Similar to Solyndra, TenKsolar employed a unique system architecture that utilized a reflective backsheet to increase performance. Critically, in 2015 the company shifted from their original inverters to a new micro-inverter-based design, and with it received an additional $25MM private equity funding round from a group led by Goldman Sachs. From a 2017 Greentech Media article[96]:

TenK had a number of good design ideas but "should have focused on one or two of those ideas," according to sources, who acknowledged the difficulty of popularizing a unique solar panel. GTM Research solar analysts and tenKsolar partners appeared to genuinely like the company's technology. Price point was a big issue, but in the end, inverter choices hastened tenKsolar's downfall.

Developers and project owners ran into major problems with TenKsolar and Solyndra, and those issues have persisted long after the two companies folded. After ceasing operations, it was nearly impossible to change out defective components. With such unique designs, you couldn't switch out one panel or inverter for another brand, as you can with other standard products, without having to replace the entire system.

In both cases, and like many companies, Solyndra and TenKsolar simply bet on the wrong technology. The cheapest solution to a problem usually wins. Increasingly affordable prices for crystalline silicon and string inverters led to the companies'

---

[96] https://www.greentechmedia.com/articles/read/sources-ten-k-solar-winding-down-operations-after-a-series-of-field-failure

inability to compete, and its products were priced out of the market. Focusing on simplicity, and ultimately compatibility, was the winning strategy.

Picking Winners & Losers

Many in the anti-renewables camp believe that the government shouldn't subsidize or provide loan guarantees to individual companies within the industry, but there are plenty of counterpoints. For one, look at the substantial subsidies given to the agriculture industry in 2019 to offset the Trump administration's tariffs. According to *The Los Angeles Times*, most of the $28 billion in bailouts ladled out to cover farm losses from the president's self-inflicted trade war likely didn't go to mom-and-pop farms, but big agribusiness operations with multi-million-dollar annual revenues. Most of them are major beneficiaries of federal crop support programs that steer billions in subsidies and low-priced crop insurance.[97]

Look at the massive subsidies provided to the fossil fuel and nuclear industries.

The United States government offers these tax subsidies to the fossil fuel industry as an incentive to produce energy domestically. These subsidies include both direct incentives to corporations as well as tax benefits to the fossil fuel industry. According to the Environmental and Energy Study Institute, "Conservative estimates put U.S. direct subsidies to the fossil fuel industry at roughly $20 billion per year; with 20 percent currently allocated to coal and 80 percent to natural gas and crude oil. European Union subsidies are estimated to a total of 55 billion euros annually."

---

[97] https://www.latimes.com/business/hiltzik/la-fi-hiltzik-trump-farm-bailout-20190528-story.html

It's true that other green-energy companies received loans or loan guarantees from the Obama administration and then ran into financial difficulty and had to declare bankruptcy. They include this convenient list, courtesy of *The Daily Signal*, an online publication of The Heritage Foundation, a Koch-funded think tank, and conservative lobbying group:[98]

- Evergreen Solar ($25 million)
- SpectraWatt ($500,000)
- Solyndra ($535 million)
- EnerDel's subsidiary Ener1 ($118.5 million)
- Abound Solar ($400 million)
- A123 Systems ($279 million)
- Willard and Kelsey Solar Group ($700,981)
- Raser Technologies ($33 million)
- Energy Conversion Devices ($13.3 million)
- Mountain Plaza, Inc. ($2 million)
- Olsen's Crop Service and Olsen's Mills Acquisition Company ($10 million)
- Range Fuels ($80 million)
- Thompson River Power ($6.5 million)
- Stirling Energy Systems ($7 million)
- Azure Dynamics ($5.4 million)
- Satcon ($3 million)
- Konarka Technologies Inc. ($20 million)
- Beacon Power ($43 million)

This may *seem* like a long list, but for anyone who knows anything about emerging technologies, until a promising and potentially dominant industry codifies it's perfectly normal to have many failures. That's what progress is all about!

---

[98] https://www.dailysignal.com/2012/10/18/president-obamas-taxpayer-backed-green-energy-failures/

For example, in the United States today the auto industry has the "Big Four" automakers —Ford, Chrysler, GM, and now Tesla. That industry was well established and, except during the 2008 Great Recession, had provided investors with a solid investment. But when the industry was emerging during the early 20th century, there were *hundreds* of automobile companies that promoted a variety of technologies.[99]

One of the most successful of the early auto companies was the Stanley Motor Carriage Company, based near Boston, Massachusetts. Their cars were *steam-powered*. And they were very good cars; in 1906 a Stanley Steamer set the world record for fastest mile in an automobile (28.2 seconds, at a top speed of 127 mph). This record was not broken by any other automobile until 1911.

Why did the Stanley Steamer disappear in 1924? The internal-combustion gasoline engine was cheaper to manufacture and when equipped with an electric starter, much easier to operate. In 1924, a Ford Model T cost $500, while a Stanley 740D sedan cost $3,950.

We saw the same phenomenon in Silicon Valley in the 1990s during the dot-com bubble. Between 1990 and 1997, the percentage of households in the United States owning computers soared, as computer ownership progressed from luxury to necessity. This marked the shift to the Information Age, an economy based on information technology. New digital tech companies were founded as quickly as entrepreneurs could find office space, and there was a climate of "irrational exuberance." But the bubble burst and between 2000 and 2004 hundreds of companies went bankrupt. By the end of the downturn in October 2002, stocks had lost $5 trillion in market capitalization since the peak in March 2002.[100]

---

[99] You can Google "list of failed automobile companies" - the list is extremely long.
[100] https://www.myvoleo.com/blog/year-2002-stock-market-crash

While many self-professed experts like to scoff at the explosion of dot-com companies, the words of Fred Wilson, a venture capitalist who funded many dot-com companies and reportedly lost 90% of his net worth when the bubble burst, are worth repeating. In his 2016 article for VentureBeat, "Here's what the future of bitcoin looks like—and it's bright," Jacob Donnelly quoted Wilson:

"A friend of mine has a great line. He says 'Nothing important has ever been built without irrational exuberance.' Meaning that you need some of this mania to cause investors to open up their pocketbooks and finance the building of the railroads or the automobile or aerospace industry or whatever. And in this case, much of the capital invested was lost, but also much of it was invested in a very high throughput backbone for the Internet, and lots of software that works, and databases and server structure. All that stuff has allowed what we have today, which has changed all our lives... that's what all this speculative mania built."[101]

SunEdison & Hubris

SunEdison was once touted by the media to someday be the world's largest energy developer, and that belief was not unfounded. In 2013, SunEdison reported that they completed over 500MW of projects. They quickly became the third-largest energy developer - behind major companies First Solar and SunPower. They remained in this spot through 2014 despite doubling their installed capacity (1,048 MW). Many felt confident that 2015 could be the year that SunEdison would claim the #1 spot. Unfortunately, the year panned out very differently.

---

[101] Donnelly, Jacob (February 14, 2016). "Here's what the future of bitcoin looks like—and it's bright." *VentureBeat.*

In the third quarter of 2015, SunEdison began experiencing liquidity issues. They couldn't secure financing to complete all their intended solar and wind developments. Their first action was to scale back plans to accommodate the installation of between 2.15 - 2.25GW. However, this wasn't enough. New projects being developed in India and Hawaii failed because they did not secure sufficient funding. There was a lack of money to start projects, continue construction, and, in a few cases, complete grid interconnection.

Ultimately, SunEdison entered into Chapter 11 bankruptcy despite receiving $300 million in Debtor-in-Possession funding from investors. At the time of that announcement, PV Tech speculated that "the sum is close to a figure that would possibly allow the company to carry out enough project completions through 2016 and sufficient liquidity for operations to exit bankruptcy down the line. However, such is the complexity of SunEdison's financial operations, lawsuits, and debts, not least the position of its two yield co businesses, that expectations at this point of a quick exit seem remote." They were right.

"SunEdison had a balance sheet that is way out of line with any other solar company," said Shayle Kann, senior vice president and renewable energy research firm GTM Research. "The projects themselves are good. They just bought too much too quickly."[102]

DC Power & Other Ponzi Schemes

In most industries, you'll run into people like Jeff and Paulette Carpoff, founders of DC Power. They hatched the largest financial fraud scheme in Cleantech history,[103] bilking investors for over $1 billion.

---

[102] https://www.reuters.com/article/us-sunedison-inc-bankruptcy/solar-developer-sunedison-in-bankruptcy-as-aggressive-growth-plan-unravels-idUSKCN0XI1TC
[103] And U.S. Eastern District of California history.

According to a 2020 Forbes article,[104] their scam involved building and leasing portable solar-powered lighting and communications towers primarily for sporting and live events. Between 2011 and 2018 DC Power attracted billions in investment from financiers with the promise of juicy returns and federal investment tax credits.

DC claimed to have built 17,000 of these solar lighting and communication systems, but only 6,000 were ever manufactured. Using what investigators claimed to be "smoke and mirrors" they sold the same equipment again and again to new buyers, reportedly scraping old VIN stickers and replacing them with new ones.

DC couldn't lease out equipment that didn't exist, but the Carpoffs paid proceeds to old investors from new investor cash. Groups like Progressive Insurance Co., East West Bancorp, and Valley National Bancorp were victims. Berkshire Hathaway took a $377 million bath tied to the reversal of investment tax credits it had claimed against fake assets.

The Carpoffs enjoyed that sweet Ponzi lifestyle while it lasted. A federal investigation had turned up cars, jets, real estate, and jewels. At auction, the Carpoffs' collection of more than 140 automobiles fetched $8.3 million. Highlights included a 1969 Plymouth Road Runner and Burt Reynolds' 1978 Pontiac Trans-Am. They even owned a semi-pro baseball team. They also held stakes in a Napa Valley winery and the Seagrape Villa at the Four Seasons Resort of St. Kitts (for which they paid $5.375 million cash) – just a few of the couple's 20 some properties around the globe. They hired Pitbull for a holiday party and owned a $782,000 luxury box at the under-construction Las Vegas Raiders stadium.

---

[104] https://www.forbes.com/sites/christopherhelman/2020/01/27/solar-power-ponzi-couple-pleads-guilty-in-billion-dollar-fraud/#5e76f10b1153

The Carpoffs' biggest unsecured creditor was Chip Ganassi, a Nascar driver whose team was owed $4.3 million by one-time sponsor DC Solar.

More than 700 of the solar units were auctioned off last year. Federal investigators have seized $120 million in assets so far and returned $500 million to the US Treasury.

Another less-publicized Ponzi scheme involved a small wind developer in the Midwest. From the Minnesota District Attorney's press release of the founder's conviction:[105]

Renewable Energy SD, LLC ("RESD"), a wind energy company headquartered in Excelsior, Minnesota ... marketed and sold wind turbines, as well as wind turbine installation and maintenance services, as a way for customers to save money by reducing or eliminating their energy expenses. RESD's customers were predominantly farmers who owned and operated farms in Minnesota, Wisconsin, and Iowa. From approximately 2010 through 2013, [RESD founder Shawn Robert] Dooling devised and executed a scheme to defraud his customers by falsely representing that for an agreed-upon contract price, RESD would build and maintain wind energy turbines on customers' land. However, in reality, Dooling spent his customers' money on personal expenses and diverted their money to pay for other customers' projects.

As part of the scheme, Dooling told customers that he would send a portion of their money to a third-party manufacturer as a down payment to reserve a specific wind turbine. Then, when the wind turbine was completed and ready to be shipped, he would send the remaining portion of the money to the manufacturer to complete the purchase. Dooling furthered his scheme by lying to customers about the status of their orders and told customers that RESD's failure to deliver the wind turbines was due to manufacturer

---

[105] https://www.justice.gov/usao-mn/pr/federal-jury-convicts-founder-wind-energy-company-multi-million-dollar-fraud-scheme

delays. As a result of his scheme, more than 70 customers paid a combined total of more than $13 million to Dooling and his company and never received the promised wind turbines or a refund of their money. Dooling withdrew approximately $2 million from RESD's bank accounts over the course of the scheme for his personal use, including luxury automobile purchases, travel, and college tuition payments for his son.

Suffice to say that clean energy is not unique – bad actors exist here as they do in other industries. It's partly the job of other cleantech companies to self-police misconduct because it reflects poorly on the rest of the industry and provides ammunition to opponents. This is not just the responsibility of trade organizations, but everyone to make sure cleantech is well-positioned for success, despite the transgressions of a few bad actors.

It's fair to ask…. What are the risks of energy itself? Are solar, wind, and geothermal energy safer and cleaner than oil, coal, and natural gas?

To answer that, our next chapter will review the risks associated with all types of fuels.

Trust Yourself

In 2012, my company, IPS Solar, was responding to changes in the marketplace that required us to either learn or face obsolescence. At that time, I teamed up with a local broker with whom I'd developed some rapport. We jointly worked on a growing portfolio of small commercial projects, but I could tell that something wasn't quite right. As conversations that seemed very straightforward started to wander and waffle, my bullshit meter ticked upwards. Unfortunately, I didn't listen to my inner voice fast enough, and we found ourselves at the altar with our clients, and no money to execute. Excuses fizzled out, one after the other, over months, and eventually, my reputation cracked, even though I'd delivered on my promises.

We dropped the relationship and moved on with other partners, but that issue caused us to lose respect. My career has been spotted with such failures. Luckily, the wins have outweighed the losses. Having a selective memory is important, but it's not always possible. Each of us has had those debilitating, ego-killing moments—the ones that sting so badly, paralysis can keep us from moving forward.

Often, it's not actual failure but the chance or perception of negative things happening that packs the biggest punch. I have my share of anxiety, and a lot of people do. It's important to realize you're never alone when it comes to mental health. If issues become too overwhelming seek out help proactively, be honest with those close to you about your challenges. No one wins when we internalize stress and negativity.

The other lesson I learned is that when entering into critical relationships, either with partners, suppliers or clients, make sure you do your homework on the counterparty and have a contingency plan should things turn south. This is especially important when dealing with money. Listen to your intuition when considering the question: "Will this person show up at closing with a check, and will those funds materialize in my account as promised?"

Clean energy is littered with failures, and solar in particular. Do your due diligence on the front end. Check references. Rely on your team of trusted advisers. Get a good attorney involved on the front end.[106]

---

[106] During the editing process my friend and personal attorney added this somewhat self-serving statement. Solid advice though so I left it in. Thanks Matt!

Irrational Exuberance

In more than a few instances I've found myself on the wrong side of irrational exuberance, where my drive outstripped my subject knowledge. This can be very dangerous. Be cautious, especially after times of success, to not drop your guard around good process. This was the case for me when we entered a new market in 2018, spending time and money without fully understanding important nuances. While calculated risk can and should be a good thing, uncalculated risk can be a predecessor to bad outcomes.

Our land development team was operating at an extremely high level, having just secured more land in Illinois (the country's biggest boom-bust community solar market) than anyone else in our industry. Riding that high, we set out to develop utility and smaller distributed solar projects in a new state. With little more than a hunch, I sent one of our team members to acquire farmland. They spent hundreds of hours developing and closing leads; we even gathered to celebrate his success.

A few weeks later, ready to submit interconnection paperwork, we contacted the interconnecting authority and the project queue had grown five-fold in just several months, crowding us out of the market. I felt terrible; what words could possibly convey my regret? A royal fuckup.

We're all human; miscalculations are and should be a forgivable offense. The primary lesson I learned here was to be especially careful when your actions directly affect other people. To this day, it's still one of my greatest regrets.

Failure is a natural part of life and a natural outcome of risk. It's not *if* you fail but *when*, and how you react. The worst response to failure is turning inward. When failing, fail fast and fail with selective memory. Don't dwell on losing but dwell purposefully on why you lost, then use that lesson as an opportunity for growth.

One of the best pieces of advice I've heard is "get to '*no*' as fast as possible." That means you're figuring out all the ways shit can hit the fan *before* things get too far down the road. I love that mentality. When you communicate like this with your stakeholders everyone's on the same page: we might not know all the answers, but we're going to try, and if it doesn't work, then we're going to try and find that out as quickly as possible.

Conversely, playing it safe either maintains the status quo or, more likely, causes you to fall behind as others surge forward.[107] Calculated risk is essential to growth. Professionally, pushing outside of your comfort zone creates the opportunity to reach new heights.

---

[107] It was at this precise moment in the book that I realized comma-use had gotten out of control.

7. Lifecycle Costs

Over the millennia, humans have harnessed energy to survive. In prehistory, we mastered fire, then sailed with the wind, harvested whale oil, and more. All energy comes at a cost, and no sources are created equal. In present day, how do we weigh the costs and benefits of adopting one form over another?

Wood was semi-renewable. You could replant deforested areas, and with good land management have more fuel in ten or twenty years (but we don't to do it). Then came coal, oil, and their various related products. All of them were extracted from the ground, and they originated with organic material that had been buried for millions of years. These fuels are non-renewable; their supply under the earth's surface of the earth is finite. Once they're burned, they're gone forever.

More recently we invented biofuels. These are defined as transportation fuels made from biomass materials, such as corn. These fuels, which include ethanol and biodiesel, are usually blended with petroleum fuels (gasoline and diesel fuel), but they can also be used on their own. They work, but it seems wasteful to grow food only to turn it into gas for your minivan. Roughly 40 percent of all U.S. corn is turned into ethanol. It's "renewable," but at a steep price.

For millions of years, humans turned to these second-generation energy sources because we were incapable of directly capturing and utilizing the most abundant energy sources: sunlight, wind, and water. Over the past few decades, however, this has started to shift.

Every form of energy comes at a price. To capture wind power, you need to manufacture efficient turbines and site them correctly. If you want coal you've got to dig in the right places. To convert sunlight into energy you need the proper technology and tools. There are risks associated with every form of energy.

The Costs of Fossil Fuels

Coal, crude oil, and natural gas are all considered fossil fuels because they were formed from the fossilized, buried remains of plants and animals that lived millions of years ago. Because of their origins, fossil fuels have a high carbon content, which is released into the air when the fuel is burned.

We know there are huge risks and costs to fossil fuels. They are too many to elucidate in this book, but here are just a few, as outlined by the Union of Concerned Scientists:[108]

Coal Mining

Coal is a solid, carbon-heavy rock existing in four main varieties differentiated largely by carbon content: lignite, sub-bituminous, bituminous, and anthracite. Found in abundance in states including Wyoming, West Virginia, Kentucky, and Pennsylvania, nearly all of the coal burned in the United States

---

[108] https://www.ucsusa.org/clean-energy/coal-and-other-fossil-fuels/hidden-cost-of-fossils#12

is sub-bituminous or bituminous. In terms of carbon content and the heat energy they can produce, these coal types are average. Regardless of variety, however, all coal is "dirty," and it's the most carbon-intensive fossil fuel we can burn.

Coal mining is dangerous work. According to the Mine Safety and Health Administration, fatalities at underground coal mine sites in the United States totaled 77 from 2010 to 2013, including a 2010 explosion at the Upper Big Branch coal mine in West Virginia that killed 29 miners.

Surface coal mining is a significant polluter. Aside from destroying streams and entire mountaintops, strip mines poison local drinking water sources with toxic chemicals including selenium, arsenic, manganese, lead, iron, and hydrogen sulfide.

A Harvard University study found that among workers, surface mining practices produced lung, cardiovascular, and kidney diseases—such as diabetes and hypertension—and an elevated occurrence of low birth rate and preterm births.

Fortunately, despite the desperate efforts by fossil fuel advocates and extremist politicians to turn back the clock to the 19th century, coal-fired power plants continue to close. Future demand for coal is expected to fall significantly as free-market forces embrace less costly renewable energy sources. In 2020, it is now cheaper to build new wind and solar projects than to operate *existing* coal facilities.

Oil Extraction

Crude oil, or petroleum (literally "rock oil" in Latin), is a liquid mixture of hydrocarbons that formed underground under high pressure from plants and animals that lived millions of years ago. It's accessed by drilling on land or at sea, or by strip mining, in the case of oil shale and tar sands oil.

Hydraulic fracturing ("fracking") is an oil extraction method that's become increasingly popular in North America. It uses massive quantities of water, so much that the vast underground aquifers in fracking states are in jeopardy of depletion and significant pollution. Fracking also uses toxic chemicals; a report by the US House of Representatives Committee on Energy and Commerce found that, from 2005 to 2009, fourteen oil and gas companies used 780 million gallons of hydraulic fracturing products containing 750 chemicals and other components.

Peer-reviewed research has found a link between certain severe health issues and individuals exposed to these chemical compounds. An exhaustive study by the Natural Resources Defense Council concluded that fracking significantly increased the probability of workers and community members enduring respiratory problems, nervous system disorders, birth defects, blood disorders, and cancer.[109]

The main component of natural gas, methane is a powerful greenhouse gas, and it's released during the drilling process. It's burned off in a process called "flaring," and the World Bank estimates that 5.3 trillion cubic feet of natural gas, the equivalent of 25 percent of total US consumption, is flared annually worldwide, generating some 400 million tons of unnecessary carbon dioxide emissions.

Oil spills are common and incredibly destructive. The last big one, the BP *Deepwater Horizon* spill in 2010, dumped approximately 134 million gallons of oil into the Gulf of Mexico, and about 1,300 miles of the US Gulf Coast from Texas to Florida were coated with oil. The oil company BP was compelled to pay $65 billion in compensation to people who relied on the Gulf for their livelihoods.

---

[109] https://www.nrdc.org/media/2014/141216

Burning Fossil Fuels

This risk of burning fossil fuels is so significant; it's beyond obvious to point it out. There are still plenty of people out there who, similar to flat earthers, refuse to accept overwhelming scientific evidence. In 2014, approximately 78 percent of US global warming emissions were energy-related carbon dioxide emissions. Of this, approximately 42 percent was from oil and other liquids, 32 percent from coal, and 27 percent from natural gas. The use of fossil fuels in transportation contributes almost 30 percent of all US global warming emissions.[110]

According to NASA, "human activities are changing the natural greenhouse. Over the last century, the burning of fossil fuels like coal and oil has increased the concentration of atmospheric carbon dioxide (CO_2)." The Intergovernmental Panel on Climate Change, a group of 1,300 independent scientific experts from countries around the world who meet under the auspices of the United Nations, have concluded there's a more than 95 percent probability that over the past fifty years, human-produced greenhouse gases such as carbon dioxide, methane, and nitrous oxide have caused most of the observed increase in Earth's temperatures.[111]

The list goes on and on... air pollution, destruction of natural resources, health hazards, groundwater poisoning. For centuries, fossil fuels have been plentiful and relatively cheap, but their cost to our quality of life has risen to an unsustainable level.

---

[110] https://www.ucsusa.org/clean-energy/coal-and-other-fossil-fuels/hidden-cost-of-fossils
[111] https://climate.nasa.gov/causes/

The Costs of Clean Energy

Are renewable energy technologies risk-free? Not necessarily. It's important to compare the true costs of clean energy with incumbent industries to understand whether our current efforts are well placed.

Solar Energy

Solar panels and their associated hardware are manufactured products, and manufacturing inherently involves consuming energy and electricity. Workers are exposed to some risks. As the Occupational Safety and Health Administration (OSHA) has pointed out, workers in the solar energy industry are potentially exposed to a variety of serious hazards including electric shock, falls, arc flashes (which include arc flash burn and blast hazards), and thermal burn hazards that can cause injury and death. Solar energy employers connected to the grid are covered by the electric power generation, transmission, and distribution standards, and therefore are required to implement the safe work practices and worker training requirements of OSHA's Electric Power Generation, Transmission, and Distribution Standard.

Another hazard of solar power is the risks involved with installation, usually on rooftops, which are dangerous places to work. States including California have imposed strict safety regulations on solar installation companies.

Those risks don't compare with getting black lung disease. As the National Census of Fatal Occupational Injuries by the US Bureau of Labor Statistics reported, mining has long been one of the most dangerous occupations in the world, with some of the worst workplace disasters in history having been mine explosions or collapses. Today, while improved safety regulations and technology have drastically reduced the likelihood of death on the job, mining machine operators still suffer a fatality rate over three times the national rate.[112]

Drilling for oil and gas offshore is also one of this nation's most dangerous professions. The risks are especially high because workers are on shift for an average of twelve hours a day, working with highly combustible materials on dangerous platforms where cranes swing heavy equipment constantly overhead.[113]

As for solar panels themselves, as manufactured products with a service life, eventually, they're going to have to be recycled. For example, as *The Verge* reported in 2018, in November 2016, the Environment Ministry of Japan warned that by 2040 the country will produce 800,000 tons of solar waste, and the recycling capacity didn't yet exist. The International Renewable Energy Agency estimated that there were already 250,000 metric tons of solar panel waste worldwide and that this number would grow to 78 million by 2050. "That's an amazing amount of growth," said Mary Hutzler, a senior fellow at the Institute for Energy Research. "It's going to be a major problem."[114]

It's a problem we can plan for and solve—assuming we have the political will, and people realize the overall environmental costs of solar power are far less than fossil fuels.

Many solar panel manufacturers are already trying to maximize the amount of recyclable content in PV modules. Traditional silicon solar modules are primarily composed of glass, plastic, and aluminum. These materials can be recycled in mass quantities at minimal cost. So, in that way, solar modules contain a high level of recyclable material. However, issues arise from the costly and time-consuming process required to recycle relevant parts of PV modules.

---

[112] https://www.bls.gov/news.release/pdf/cfoi.pdf
[113] http://content.time.com/time/nation/article/0,8599,1984296,00.html
[114] https://www.theverge.com/2018/10/25/18018820/solar-panel-waste-chemicals-energy-environment-recycling

Current recycling processes involves removing the aluminum frames and separating glass from the panels. This is followed by intense thermal processing at 500 degrees Celsius necessary to melt down small plastic components that allow for easier separation of the panels' cells. Lastly, recycling centers have to deal with the silicon components of the panel. Silicon wafers must be etched away and smelted into slabs. These reusable silicone slabs are said to make use of roughly 85% of the total silicon components. Therefore, the reality remains that solar panels are not entirely recyclable in their current state.

The seemingly biggest challenge facing PV module recycling is access to specialized equipment. The process requires expensive machinery and hours of labor. There's no question that the industry has some work to do in determining a streamlined process and figuring out the best solutions to optimize future technology for a recyclable afterlife.

Wind Power

As tall wind turbines appear in increasing numbers across rural landscapes, skeptics are going to great lengths to point out both real and imagined drawbacks. Although wind turbines have a minuscule impact on the environment compared to fossil fuel power plants, concerns have been raised over the noise produced by rotor blades and deaths of birds and bats that fly into the rotors (avian/bat mortality).

The most common complaint is the noise, both of the "swoosh" of the blades sweeping through the air and the mechanical "grind" of the generator itself. As Roy D. Jeffery, MD and colleagues concluded in their report "Adverse health effects of industrial wind turbines," if sited too close to residents, industrial wind turbines (IWTs) may be psychologically damaging to some people. This harm can be avoided if IWTs are situated at an appropriate distance from residents. A lack of adequately protective siting guidelines can result in people exposed to IWTs presenting these psychological symptoms to their family physicians in increasing numbers.[115]

In recent years, turbine designers have made changes to reduce the noise. As they have become more efficient, more of the wind is converted into rotational torque and less into acoustic noise. Additionally, proper insulating materials can help minimize noise impacts.

As for bird strikes, government agencies and the wind industry are conducting research into relevant bird and bat behavior, collisions, mitigation measures, and appropriate study design protocols. In addition, at existing and proposed wind energy sites, project developers are required to collect data through monitoring efforts.

In offshore areas, concerns have been raised by the fishing industry. The first offshore wind farm in the United States was constructed off the coast of Rhode Island's Block Island in 2016. Since then, there's been wind turbine construction or plans proposed in Connecticut and Massachusetts, and elsewhere along the Eastern Seaboard in New Jersey, New York, and Maryland. Commercial fishermen have expressed concern over impact to fishing grounds, and a group of fishermen filed a lawsuit against the federal government in response to a proposed wind farm in Long Island. "You do have to realize we have a new industry going in a place where another industry has existed, and the status quo is always safer than the unknown," said Brian Hooker a marine biologist at the US Bureau of Ocean Energy Management. Meanwhile, research is ongoing into the actual measurable impact offshore wind farms may have on the fishing industry.[116]

---

[115] https://www.ncbi.nlm.nih.gov/pmc/articles/PMC3653647/
[116] https://energynews.us/2019/04/17/northeast/in-northeast-more-research-needed-on-offshore-winds-impact-on-fishing/

Electric Battery Recycling

Many may be surprised to know that some of the earliest practical automobiles were powered by batteries and electric motors. In the United States, the first electric car was developed in 1890 by William Morrison of Des Moines, Iowa; the vehicle was a six-passenger wagon capable of reaching a top speed of 14 mph. By the turn of the century, electric vehicles had several advantages over their steam or gas-powered competitors: They were super quiet, easy to drive, and started instantly. They sold well—in the United States at that time, 40 percent of automobiles were powered by steam, 38 percent by electricity, and only 22 percent by gasoline.

The fatal flaw with early electric cars was the battery technology. Car batteries of the traditional lead-acid design were heavy, took time to charge, had limited range, and performed poorly in cold weather. Overtaken by cheaper gas-powered cars that could go much farther in any weather, by 1920 production of electric cars had nearly ceased.

The lithium-ion battery has revolutionized the electric car industry. First commercialized by Sony and Asahi Kasei in 1991, compared to lead-acid batteries, lithium-ion batteries are smaller, lighter in weight, and can produce more power for extended periods of time. Automakers quickly began designing electric vehicles using lithium-ion batteries, and the market segment steadily gained ground.

In 2016, the number of electric cars in the world passed the two-million mark and the International Energy Agency estimated there would be 140 million electric cars globally by 2030 if countries meet Paris climate agreement targets.

Electric cars also found political favor. In 2016, the British and French governments committed to outlaw the sale of gas and diesel-powered cars by 2040, and carmakers like Audi and Volvo pledged to only sell electric or hybrid vehicles by the early 2020s. In China, the world's largest auto market, regulators are reportedly weighing a target for 60 percent of all automobiles sold in the country to run on electricity by 2035.

This sounds like good news for the climate fight —but what's the plan for these batteries after their useful life?

Lithium-ion batteries are not without risk. If damaged, they can emit toxic gases. The core ingredients including lithium and cobalt are finite, and extraction from the earth—just like mining any other mineral resource—can lead to water pollution and environmental damage.

Proper recycling is key, but as Joey Gardiner wrote in *The Guardian*, in the European Union as few as five percent of lithium-ion batteries are currently recycled. And according to Ajay Kochhar, CEO of Canadian battery recycling startup Li-Cyclem, the electric vehicle boom could leave 11 million tons of spent lithium-ion batteries in need of recycling between now and 2030.

But it's not all doom and gloom of course. The low rate of battery recycling is largely in the consumer electronics sector—phones and laptops. Car batteries are different. Marc Grynberg, chief executive of Belgian battery and recycling giant Umicore, predicts "car producers will be accountable for the collection and recycling of spent lithium-ion batteries.... Given their sheer size, batteries cannot be stored at home and landfilling is not an option."[117]

Entrepreneurs like the Footprint Project's Will Heegard are finding unique ways to address the battery waste issue. A registered paramedic, Will responded with the International Medical Corps to Typhoon Haiyan in the Philippines and deployed solar refrigeration in West Africa during the Ebola outbreak.

---

[117] https://www.theguardian.com/sustainable-business/2017/aug/10/electric-cars-big-battery-waste-problem-lithium-recycling

During his work, he noticed that most recovery efforts were utilizing costly and dirty diesel generators for critical power.

With clean energy costs and availability improving significantly, Footprint was born to provide recovering communities with better solutions. According to their website, the organization displaces fossil fuel generators with solar plus storage in austere emergency and disaster recovery contexts. They help responders deploy clean technologies that both save lives now and support resilient recovery later. They partner with relief agencies interested in reducing power outages, cutting fuel costs, and improving energy access for their beneficiaries.

Footprint's portable power stations utilize refurbished car batteries, primarily from older Nissan Leaf's, to store and regulate power. After thousands of cycles, these batteries are still operating at 70% or more of their original capacity. The wide availability and cost-effectiveness of older batteries make them a great fit for disaster recovery systems. Footprint is scaling their operations to address relief in a myriad of contexts, including post-hurricane Puerto Rico, remote coronavirus testing facilities, tornado recovery in Tennessee, flood relief in the Midwest, and elsewhere.

In summary, as you find your way in the clean energy industry, you'll see that while the unstoppable trend is toward growth, there will be challenges. These challenges will be produced by the very nature of growth—just like any other major transformation we've seen throughout history—and will also come from opponents who have deeply entrenched political and financial interests in preserving the status quo. But where there are challenges, there are opportunities for entrepreneurialism to solve problems.

8. Building A Foundation

"If you're not learning, then you're stagnant. If you're stagnant, then you're not evolving and the business isn't progressing."

- Seth Rollins, American professional wrestler

"Learning and innovation go hand in hand. The arrogance of success is to think that what you did yesterday will be sufficient for tomorrow."

- William Pollard, English Quaker writer, and recorded minister.

"Successful people are great learners."

- Dr. T. P. Chia, Singaporean former political prisoner.

Having a basic knowledge of clean energy's technology and business landscape is important for career-seekers. If you see your future in this industry the next step is to build a foundation from which you can launch your career or transition.

In the beginning, no one starts with VIP offices, eighteen-hole power meetings, and steakhouse dinners – it's all about hustle. Nothing is handed to you, and the sooner you understand that getting anywhere in life requires monumental work ethic, the better off you'll be.

That being said, the very beginning of your venture into clean energy (or any other industry) may not require a Herculean effort. It will require you to take the first step, and that begins with knowing who you are and what you have to offer.

Value

When you embark on any clean energy career, whether it's washing Tesla's rolling off the assembly line or designing their advanced battery technology, you are going to get paid in relation to the value you can create. Washing cars is a relatively low-value job that most anyone could do, and therefore you can expect to be paid accordingly. Designing the chemistry for advanced batteries is a highly specialized position where you will be paid much more. And if you're an executive at Tesla, in charge of an entire department of engineers your salary is likely in the stratosphere.

Your value in the job marketplace is commonly defined by three metrics:

(Please note this discussion applies only to readers who want to work for an employer, in a conventional sense. It *doesn't* apply to entrepreneurs who want to start and run their own business. For entrepreneurs, no rules apply. A successful entrepreneur can be anyone, with virtually any level of education or experience. The list of billionaire entrepreneurs with no college degree is long, and includes Steve Jobs, Bill Gates, Mark Zuckerberg, Steve Jobs, Travis Kalanick.... you get the idea. Chapter 10 expands on entrepreneurialism, beyond that there are a million books specific to that topic.)

1. Education

It's a reliable rule that the more formal education you have, the more money you're going to be paid.

The seven levels of education are:

1. No high school diploma. This is the lowest level, where no one wants to be.
2. High school diploma or GED. For almost any job, this is the minimum requirement.
3. Two-year certificate or associate's degree.
4. Bachelor's degree.
5. Master's degree.
6. Professional degree (MD, lawyer, etc.)
7. Doctoral degree (Ph.D.)

In general, the higher on the scale you are, the more you'll be paid because you will qualify for higher-paying jobs.

According to data from the U.S. Bureau of Labor Statistics (BLS), as education levels rise, two things are true: your earnings increase and your risk of unemployment decreases. Grouping workers by education level, statistics show those with more education have higher earnings and lower rates of unemployment than those with less education.

For example, in 2015 (the most recent BLS data), workers with a professional degree had the highest median weekly earnings ($1,730) and lowest unemployment rate (1.5 percent) of all groups. That's more than triple the weekly earnings ($493) and less than one-fifth the unemployment rate (8.0 percent) of the bottom tier—workers without a high school diploma.[118]

2. Experience

When you're a college kid looking for a summer job, employers don't expect you to have experience. You could get

---

[118] US BLS. https://www.bls.gov/careeroutlook/2016/data-on-display/education-matters.htm

hired as an intern at a solar company with zero prior experience; all you need is a good attitude, passion, and the willingness to take direction.

Sales positions are often available with little or no prior experience (as was the case with IPS and me). That's because salespeople primarily earn paychecks by selling, and most companies will give someone a shot at selling for a probationary period. After that, if you're not meeting expectations, you'll be back on the street job searching. Salespeople can be very successful, but—as I'll discuss in the next section—being a salesperson can limit your mobility into other areas of business.

The higher up you go on the employment ladder, the more experience you're going to need. The level of experience required for a job is very important in two areas: technical qualifications and management responsibility.

For example, in technical qualifications, if you want to work with live household or industrial electricity, you must have your electrician's license. Laws regulating electricians vary by state. In California, for example, all electricians who make connections of greater than 100-volt amps working for C-10 contractors need a C-10 electrical contractor license. To get a C-10 electrical contractor license in California, you must prove a minimum of four years of journeyman-level experience and pass a two-part state exam with the Contractor State License Board.

If you can't prove four years of experience, you will not qualify for your C-10 license and can't be hired for jobs requiring that license.

Every job description will include the necessary experience. Employers want to hire people who require minimal training and who can "hit the ground running" on their new job. They want people who can make a contribution and add value to the organization. Often, employers will have a particular challenge or project in mind and will look for someone who has solved that problem in the past. For example, if a wind farm developer wants to erect an offshore wind farm, and the problem they face is assessing the impact of the wind farm on marine life and birds, the company will look to hire someone with prior experience in this specific area.

Which brings us to the third and perhaps most important metric that determines your job prospects in the renewable energy industry.

3. Organizational Fit

Employers are looking for people who are the *best fit* for the job and for the organization. They want candidates whose education and experience closely match the job description, *and* they want people who align with their company culture.

Cultural fit can be arbitrary and difficult to pinpoint. Managers and executives obsess over it. In general, like other aspects of your search, it's important to do your homework. Does the organization's values seem like they match with yours? Are you passionate about what they do and how you can help? If those answers are no it's probably not a good fit on either side. Culture is a human element that's qualitative and difficult to predict.

At the very beginning, there may be no human element at all. Many larger employers use software to scan applicant resumes, screening for keywords that are included in the job description. For example, here's a typical job posting. It's from a company called Form Energy, and the position is Senior Battery Engineer.

Here's the basic description:

We are looking for a Senior Battery Engineer to aid in the product development efforts of Form Energy's long-duration energy storage system. The Senior Battery Engineer will be responsible for component integration, conceptual design, and active-area scale-up of Form Energy's core energy-storing reactor....

Then there's a bullet-point list of actual job responsibilities:

• *Propose design changes to Form Energy's electrochemical energy-storing reactor, especially relating to optimization of fluid delivery systems, mass transport, and overpotential reduction strategies....*

Finally, the qualifications are stated. This is where the most important keywords will be embedded:

- *BS (MS preferred) in Mechanical Engineering, Chemical Engineering, Materials Science, or a related field.*
- *7+ years' experience designing electrochemical energy storage or conversion systems (i.e., PEM fuel cells, SOFCs, Li-ion, alkaline batteries).*
- *Has deep practical experience with electrochemical science and systems.*
- *Direct experience working in an environment geared towards electrochemical product development or pilot electrochemical system deployment.*
- *Experience with optimizing mass transport and fluid mechanics through electrochemical systems.*
- *Experience designing experiments in an industrial research setting.*
- *Experience communicating new designs through CAD models, sketches, and design reviews is a plus.*
- *Experience with computational modeling (i.e., COMSOL, MATLAB, Python) is a plus.*[119]

---

[119]FormEnergy.https://hire.withgoogle.com/public/jobs/formenergycom/view/P_AAAAAAIAABRNN BGU4Pquqy

You can see all the relevant keywords. Resumés of successful applicants should contain a high number of matches for these words and acronyms — "electrochemical," "PEM fuel cells," "COMSOL," and others.

Transitions

In an economy with very low unemployment, like we had in 2019 and the pre-COVID 19 world of 2020, there will be very few qualified applicants for a position like this, and the company may consider you even if you fall short in a few areas. But in a time of high unemployment, like during the peak of the Great Recession in 2010 or the post-COVID 19 world of 2020, there will be a flood of qualified applicants for jobs like these, and the company will consider your application only if you're a high-quality match.

Entering the renewable energy industry from another industry, or changing career paths within the industry, is possible if you're looked upon favorably by the person making the hiring decision.

Earlier in the book, I mentioned that it can be difficult to move out of sales and into a "core" role. Salespeople who are not professionals are generally not considered part of the core business. The assumption is that a salesperson who's good at selling could sell anything—new cars, solar panels, toasters—and don't need to be involved in the core business of creating products. But if you have the right qualifications, you can go from sales into marketing, and from there ease into product development. And if you work for a small company, like a start-up, chances are everyone at the company is multitasking.

If you want to get into the renewables industry from, say, your job as a bank teller, then you'll have to start fairly low on the totem pole and work your way into your dream role. Again, it depends on how much of your education and experience can be transferred to a renewables job. If you have a bachelor's degree in Chinese Studies and you speak fluent Mandarin but have no experience in the energy sector, your skills might be needed by a cleantech company seeking to do business in China, or with a Chinese company looking to sell in the United States.

Likewise, earlier I used the example of a wind farm developer who wants to erect an offshore wind farm, and they need to hire someone with prior experience assessing the impact of wind farms on marine life and birds. The person they hire probably doesn't need to know much about how wind farms work or how to build them. But they need to be an expert in marine life and how human activity, particularly undersea structures, can disrupt it.

The larger the industry becomes, the more opportunities there will be for people who have business skills that may not directly relate to the technology of renewable energy. Let's say you're a corporate accountant by profession, and theoretically, you could be an accountant at any company in any industry. But if you like renewable energy and enjoy being in that environment, you could make a career out of doing accounting for clean energy companies.

This leads us to the next section—your unique selling proposition.

Unique Selling Proposition

When you go to the store, you buy brands you like because they have attributes that fit what you want or need. One brand of toothpaste might get your teeth whiter, another might freshen your breath, while another may have the lowest price. Brands work very hard to differentiate themselves in the marketplace. They strive to carve out an identity and stick to that identity consistently, year after year. This is called brand or product differentiation and any special qualities create their unique selling proposition.

The job market is very similar. While you need to meet minimum requirements for a job you want—just like every brand of toothpaste must get your teeth clean—it's also important that you have something extra to offer that others might not.

Everyone has a skill they're especially good at or an interest in a particular area. Even if you're not the best in the world at that thing, the fact that you're better than average can give you an important leg up. This is your unique selling proposition.

When you can combine two or more skills, then your "package" becomes even better and more difficult for a competitor to replicate. This can turn into your secret sauce—the differentiator between you and all others in your field.

For instance, coming out of college I was pretty well versed in web development, graphic design, and marketing. With that early set of skills, I was able to create compelling messages that cut through the noise, and I got my foot in the door.

Here are some basic skills that are useful in the clean energy sector:

- Math and accounting
- Communication/writing
- Social engagement
- Computer literacy
- Public speaking/presentation
- Software code writing

These are advanced skills:

- Engineering
- Financing
- Technical sales
- Management
- Information technology
- Law

Adding skills increases your marketability exponentially. As a basic exercise, if we assigned a value of 2 to the basic skills above and 4 to the advanced skills, a person with computer literacy and engineering abilities would have a "differentiator score" of 2 x 4 = 8. However, if you added creativity and management to the arsenal all of a sudden your uniqueness jumps to 2 x 2 x 4 x 4 = 64.

All of this is an oversimplified way of organizing your traits into a blueprint of who you are and what you do best. Armed with this new sense of self, you can confidently begin your journey in clean energy, knowing exactly how to deliver value for your employer or clients.

Create Your Unique Selling Proposition

As you begin your job search, take a hard look at your strengths. Take a minute to catalog your skills and create your Unique Selling Proposition:

My Basic Skills:

_____.
_____.
_____.
_____.

My Advanced Skills:

_____.
_____.
_____.
_____.

My Unique Selling Proposition:

_____.
_____.

Research the Industry

As you discover your passion and develop your unique selling proposition, the next step is to research the myriad career options at your fingertips. The beautiful part of this clean energy revolution is that there are a multitude of opportunities across the spectrum. To illustrate this point, below is a limited list of career categories that you'll see in the renewable energy industry:

Career categories in renewable energy:

- Acquisition agent
- Administrative / clerical
- Analyst
- Asset manager
- Batteries and energy storage
- Business development
- Control room operator
- Corrosion science and technology
- Customer service
- Development & project management

- Dielectric science and materials
- Education and teaching
- Electrical engineer
- Electrical maintenance
- Electrocatalysis
- Electrochemical engineering
- Electrolyzers
- Electronic devices and systems
- Electronic materials and processing
- Electronic packaging engineer
- Energy conversion
- Energy engineer
- Events and conferences
- Environmental engineer
- Executive
- Financial and accounting
- Fuel cells
- General management
- IT and software development
- Information technology
- Manufacturing
- Materials handling
- Meteorologist
- Operations and maintenance
- Planner – environmental
- Private law firm associate
- Program and project management
- Research and development
- Safety specialist
- Sales
- Sensors
- Technician
- Transportation

Here are some specific job titles in the wind power sector:

- Blade technician
- Principal engineer - wind turbine technology
- Post-doctoral fellow - power and energy research
- Installation energy program analyst
- Utilities and energy services trainee
- R&D staff member - applied spectroscopy and diagnostics for clean energy transportation
- Field service representative - power distribution
- Technical director
- Wind/blade technician II + traveling technicians
- There are many more!

For an idea of what careers or jobs exist and are in demand, take a look at various industry job boards online. The more you notice employers in search of specific job titles, the more those positions are needed. Google the following:

SEIA / Solar Energy Industries Association

The Solar Energy Industries Association (SEIA®) is committed to building, through advocacy and education, a strong solar industry to power America. As the national trade association for the U.S. solar energy industry, which employs more than 242,000 Americans, SEIA represents organizations that promote, manufacture, install, and support the development of solar energy. SEIA works with its 1,000 member companies to build jobs and diversity, champion the use of cost-competitive solar in America, remove market barriers, and educate the public on the benefits of solar energy.

On their Solar Job Board, you can manage your career online. Create an account to save jobs, store your resume and cover letters, search for jobs, and set up job alerts.

The American Wind Energy Association (AWEA)

The American Wind Energy Association (AWEA) is the national trade association for the U.S. wind industry. With thousands of wind industry members and wind policy advocates, AWEA promotes wind energy as a clean source of electricity for American consumers.

The AWEA website features a careers section and Job Search Resource Center that provides everything you need to make your resume stand out, succeed at the interview, advance your career, and navigate the digital world through social media and digital communication. If you have questions about your job search, you can ask their career experts and get the assistance you need. Their coaches make every attempt to answer your questions within one business day.

The U.S. Energy Storage Association (ESA)

This is the U.S. national trade association dedicated to energy storage, working toward a more resilient, efficient, sustainable, and affordable electricity grid, as is uniquely enabled by energy storage. With more than 190 members, ESA represents a diverse group of companies, including independent power producers, electric utilities, energy service companies, financiers, insurers, law firms, installers, manufacturers, component suppliers and integrators involved in deploying energy storage systems around the globe.

The ESA Career Center is a targeted resource that connects companies in the energy storage industry with highly qualified professionals looking to grow their careers. You can open an account and use it to manage your job searches and career development. The ESA Career Center offers services including:

- Career coaching from certified coaches with the experience, training, and expertise needed to help you achieve your career goals;
- Resume coaching. Whether you are a mid-career professional, a senior executive, or newly entering the job market, ESA experts are ready to critique your existing resume or help you craft a document that gets you noticed.
- Reference checking. Get your references checked confidentially and professionally so you can be confident your past employers are helping, not hurting, your candidacy.

DSIREUSA.org / Database of State Incentives for Renewables & Efficiency®

DSIRE is the most comprehensive source of information on incentives and policies that support renewables and energy efficiency in the United States. Established in 1995, DSIRE is operated by the N.C. Clean Energy Technology Center at N.C. State University and is funded by the U.S. Department of Energy.

While not a job listing site, DSIRE Insight's subscription services focus on distributed solar, grid modernization and energy storage, and electric vehicles, as well as customized energy policy research.

Obviously, the internet is a tremendous resource here. During the last semester of my super-senior year, I researched different industries that had some impact on climate change, of which there are many. For me, it came down to renewable energy—either wind or solar. Both technologies were growing at a 40% rate year over year. Exponential improvement is an incredible thing, as evidenced by the facts provided in the first chapter.

In 2007, solar energy's price was hovering around $4.00 per watt wholesale, and the most efficient panel available to small installation companies was about 195 watts. Doing the math, that panel cost around $800 wholesale. Today panel pricing is dropping below $.30 per watt wholesale. Many of the most efficient panels in the market are exceeding 400 watts in that same footprint.

Learning

After the research phase, you may decide that additional education is important. One of the best ways to discern this is to review job descriptions for professionals in the same position that you're seeking.

There are two primary paths regarding education: formal and informal. The formal path involves post-secondary institutions like technical colleges and universities. Maybe it's an engineering or wind turbine technician degree. Or maybe it's an MBA. Formal degrees typically offer financial aid to those who qualify and there are other grants or scholarships. Informal training typically requires less commitment with a much shorter duration. This training could take the form of introductory courses offered by third parties or industry-certified professionals, either online (mostly) or in-person.

If you decide further education is needed, definitely research the institutions or organizations that interest you. On the informal side, check for reviews or seek out those who have completed or taught courses. The veracity of these organizations is usually easy to discern. For formal education, take time and do the math of the total cost, and compare that to the earning opportunity for careers related to those degrees. The total cost should include tuition and living expenses, and the loans required to pay them off. Compare that to the income opportunity for careers in that field. How long would it take to pay down the debt? Money isn't everything; happiness should play a huge role in where you choose to focus. Although not totally necessary, think about the intersections between what makes you happy and earning potential.

Education is a tricky subject with no right or wrong answers. Marketers like Gary Vaynerchuk have gained popularity by encouraging young adults to avoid the perceived "trap" of going to college, incurring debt, and working years or even decades to pay it back. The flip side is that there's value in learning and achieving expertise in a subject, which can't always be found on the streets of hard knocks.

Knowledge Transfer with Nico Johnson

Nico Johnson is one of renewable energy's most preeminent thought leaders. As host of the influential (and often cited) podcast *Suncast*, he's interviewed hundreds of successful cleantech trailblazers. Creating over 300 episodes with now days-worth of content he's a wealth of knowledge. I had the good fortune of interviewing Nico in February 2020 where he waxed philosophical on many topics pertaining to clean energy and career success. According to Nico, the ability to transfer knowledge from one industry to another is critical for job-seekers:

My guest John Chaimanis of Kendall Investment, Episode 196, shared a piece of advice that one of his mentors had given him, and it stuck with me. He said, "you can only change one of two things: your industry or your function within an industry, but never both."

For instance, you couldn't go from telecom to solar and in telecom, you were technical sales and in solar, you got your MBA and now you're doing finance. You could go into technical sales in solar and eventually work your way into a new job from there.

Or you can stay in your industry but change roles. So maybe you go from sales to finance or engineering to sales within a given space or organization. You just wouldn't want to do both at the same time.

Martin DeBono is the current President at GAF Energy – a company that is transforming the roofing industry by integrating solar into every roof – and a 2020 Suncast interviewee. Martin's tech background at industry giants Cisco and Siebel gave him key skills in channel management that he's now translated to the growth of some of rooftop solar's most respected brands – SunPower and GAF Energy. Nico remarked that "he really learned distribution, how channel partners worked for getting routers into the world. He took that knowledge of value-added resellers and building distribution channels, and brought it to SunPower and that's what stabilized [the company's] residential and capital side of the business for the ensuing ten years."

For new entrants, Nico shared additional insight – gain core skills from somewhere else first:

Go from the macro to the micro. Learn what drives the industry and get [a] free education from big companies who can afford to give it to you. For instance, in the energy sector, go as big as possible – to Duke, Nextera, Macquarie. Pick a big company and ... learn everything you can. Just be a sponge and absorb everything so you can be a useful contributor if you move to a smaller company. Be okay with making $50,000 to $75,000 a year before you try and strike it rich as a startup.

Or join another industry all together like consumer-packaged goods, telecom, IT, or high tech. Learn how that industry works but be a specialist. Go to a company like Proctor and Gamble, get in their marketing internship program, work two to three years on their leadership rotation and jump to any industry you want, with all the credibility you could possibly desire.

Started from the Bottom Now We're Here[120]

One trend noted by Nico Johnson in the hundreds of interview hours with cleantech leaders is that the people who really excel have a willingness to work up from the bottom, often for free.

"Tara Doyle [of PV Evolution Labs] and Dylan Dupree [of CalCom Energy] both started as the front desk person, and now both have grown into significant roles at the top of their organizations. Many [leaders] find success by starting in the industry and learning as much as possible about the way different roles interact with one another. Which means, in my view, that you have to be an infinite learner. You must have a willingness to ask questions, learn from the answers and experiment."

This concept is not unique to cleantech, there are plenty of other examples. Richard Olson of the Toro Company started as a Process Engineer at 22 and is now CEO. At age 20 Chris Rondeau was a Planet Fitness front desk attendant and at 45 he is CEO. Across the business spectrum, the values are similar.

Working in lower-level positions allows you to understand the specifics of company or industry nuances. You can also network with other rising leaders from whom you can learn and grow

---

[120] I get it. It's safe to say Drake's *Started from the Bottom* is one the most over-referenced songs of the last decade but I couldn't resist.

together. It gives you the street cred for later promotion opportunities, as many companies prefer to promote from within.

Confidence

Influential magazine *Psychology Today* published an article by Ph.D. Jim Taylor[121] in which he noted that "confidence is the most important psychological contributor to performance in business because you may have all the ability in the world to accomplish a goal, but if you don't believe you have that ability, you won't do it to the fullest extent." In my 2020 interview with Nico Johnson he cited a few examples (of many) in the cleantech space:

"Mark Manson wrote an excellent book called The Subtle Art of Not Giving a Fuck. *To a certain extent, you look at a guy like Dan Shugar [cofounder of PowerLight and founder of NextTracker] and even Jigar [Shah]. They're emblematic of this idea that you just have to get good at not giving a fuck about what people say or think about you. I've found that to be universally true." – Nico Johnson*

Obviously being confident is easier said than done in most instances, especially in a realm that's new or foreign to you. There's a direct correlation between confidence and the knowledge or talent you possess in a particular area, so learn as much as you can and as quickly as you can to gain assurance. In essence, confidence is a skill. Taylor remarked:

A mistake many people make in their understanding of how confidence affects them is to believe that it is something that they either have or don't have and if they don't have it, they will never be able to get it. To the contrary, confidence is a skill that develops with awareness and practice. Think of confidence as being like a sports skill. If you practice bad technique repeatedly, you will become very

---

skilled at the bad technique and that is what will come out in competition.

Additionally, that ingrained bad technique will make it more difficult to learn new good techniques because it will be ingrained into your muscle memory. Conversely though, if you practice good technique, that is what you will ingrain and that is what will come out in competition. The same holds true for confidence. If you practice being negative, worried, and discouraging, then you will become skilled at the negativity and that pessimistic mindset will emerge when you are in an important business situation, such as a sales call or under deadline to finish a work project.

There is a distinct difference between confidence and arrogance obviously, but the line between the two is blurry. False confidence can manifest as arrogance, which can go along with being closed off to new ideas. If you don't have the expertise or are particularly self-assured in something you have no business being self-assured about, people will get turned off. It's in your best interest to be confident but open to new ways of thinking.

In whatever way you choose to express confidence make sure it's genuine. Being genuinely interested in something or someone is a powerful way to engage. On the other hand, being disingenuous is a surefire way for others to lose confidence in you, creating a negative perception or reputation that could be hard to recover from. In clean energy, if you're excited about the technology or fighting the climate crisis, typically that enthusiasm will show up in your work. This creates a positive feedback loop which drives success, and in turn more confidence.

9. Green Networking

"There are only two mistakes one can make along the road to truth; not going all the way, and not starting."

- Buddha

"Enjoy the journey and try to get better every day. And don't lose the passion and the love for what you do."

- Nadia Comaneci, gymnast, and five-time Olympic gold medalist.

"Focus on the journey, not the destination. Joy is found not in finishing an activity but in doing it."

- Greg Anderson, author.

Submitting applications blindly into the internet's abyss is not the most effective option for job seekers. A warm introduction or inside track is almost always better. But how do you do that?

Remember Evan Hynes's story from Chapter 2? He attended numerous focus events and even created a blog where he interviewed some of tech's most influential people

These activities are known more basically as *networking*, and they create opportunities not available to people scrolling on Indeed. Networking has many benefits.

Industry insight. Networking allows you to gain insight into facets of the renewable energy industry with which you may not be familiar. You'll have greater access to emerging trends, future challenges, and new ideas.

Career opportunities. While many job openings are posted publicly, others are not. Many leaders in the renewable energy industry have risen through the ranks not because they've applied for jobs but because a manager who needed a new person to fill a role thought of them and hired them. Sometimes roles are created simply because a company wants to bring a certain individual onboard, and they'll create a role for that person to fill.

Learning opportunities. Many industry organizations offer lectures, classes, and mentoring programs. You can be a beneficiary of these programs, and then as your career develops maybe you can be a contributor.

Here are a few prominent renewable energy trade associations:

United States Renewable Energy Association, LLC (USREA)

Based in Lexington, Michigan, USREA is a renewable energy advocacy group working to both educate and promote advanced technologies in the renewable energy industry. They have a blog and news service online and encourage engagement through content posted by educational, corporate, and enthusiast members alike. The association promotes advanced renewable technologies including electric aircraft, or stripping electricity directly from the air, massive energy harvesting from multiple sources, and solar/wind/wave/biomass technology, to name a few. Site news and perspective keep members informed about industry events and milestones with a core focus of renewable energy in the United States.[122]

The American Council on Renewable Energy (ACORE)

Founded in 2001, ACORE is a 501(c)(3) national nonprofit organization that unites finance, policy, and technology to accelerate the transition to a renewable energy economy.

Based in Washington D.C., the group sees itself as a central point for collaborative advocacy across the renewable energy sector. It's supported by members representing renewable energy technologies and constituencies including academic institutions, professional service firms, utilities, developers, grid technology providers, manufacturers, allied nonprofit groups, top financial institutions, and major corporate renewable energy buyers.

To fulfill its mission, ACORE seeks to convene leaders across key constituencies, educate senior officials on important policies, publish research and analysis on pressing issues, facilitate partnerships, and undertake strategic outreach on the policies and financial structures essential to renewable energy growth.[123]

The American Solar Energy Society (ASES)

Established way back in 1954, ASES is a 501(c)(3) non-profit that advocates for sustainable living and 100 percent renewable energy. Based in Boulder, Colorado, the organization shares resources, information, and events to cultivate community and power progress in the U.S. and beyond. As the U.S. section of the International Solar Energy Society (ISES), ASES works with

---

[122] https://www.usrea.org/
[123] https://acore.org/

individuals and groups around the world to accelerate the transition to global renewable energy and sustainable living.[124]

International Geothermal Association (IGA)

By setting educational standards and offering worldwide energy solutions and in-house technical support, with special support for countries in the early stages of geothermal development, the IGA strives to be the leading world authority in the research and development of geothermal energy.

Based in Bonn, Germany, the IGA connects the global geothermal community and serves as a platform for networking opportunities aimed at promoting and supporting global geothermal development. The organization comprises a wide variety of members ranging from industry to academic representatives.[125]

Women of Renewable Industries and Sustainable Energy (WRISE)

Women of Renewable Industries and Sustainable Energy[126] promotes the education, professional development, and advancement of women to achieve a strong diversified workforce and support a robust renewable energy economy.

According to a 2017 article by Greetech Media[127] "female representation within the renewable energy sector is small. In OECD[128] nations, it's estimated that only 20 percent of those

---

[124] https://www.ases.org/
[125] https://www.geothermal-energy.org/
[126] https://wrisenergy.org/
[127]https://www.greentechmedia.com/articles/read/why-its-still-important-to-talk-about-diversity-in-the-renewables-sector
[128] So, I had no idea what OECD (Organization for Economic Co-operation and Development) countries were until I ran into this article. Apparently, it's a group of 36 countries that originally formed in 1961.

employed are women. A majority work in sales and administration, followed by engineering and technical departments. Solar PV is the largest renewables sector representing female workers, followed by solar heating and cooling, wind energy, biomass, and biofuel.

Gender equality and gender diversity are very important. Good organizations understand the value of different perspectives and certainly women are tremendous leaders. But there's still a staggering amount of discrimination and harassment in the workplace; I don't pretend to be an expert on these issues but I fully support equity for all and am willing to listen and learn. WRISE offers an important platform for women to grow and improve. From their website:

Founded in 2005 as Women of Wind Energy (WoWE) and rebranded in May 2017, Women of Renewable Industries and Sustainable Energy (WRISE) is a national nonprofit with a growing presence working across the renewable energy economy with over 30 chapters and a broad purpose – to change our energy future through the actions of women. By building Community, promoting Education, and cultivating Leadership, WRISE works to recruit, retain, and advance women and inspire our members and the public to unite in raising their voices for others.

In a 2020 Suncast interview Britta von Oesen commented on the seemingly benign sexism mothers face that fathers do not:

"It's [a] question that I always just dread being asked: How do you balance work and life? How do you do all of this while being a mother?

According to Wikipedia member countries collectively comprised 62.2% of global GDP in 2017. Noticeably absent from the organization are emerging powerhouses China, India, and Brazil (and a total of zero African countries).

It bothers me for a variety of reasons. The first of which is that I'm usually speaking on panels, as an expert finance and renewable energy. Instead [of focusing on the topic] people are devoting time to discuss motherhood. I have two little girls who mean the world to me and my family is incredibly important to me...

Really [it's] the fact that it is predominantly asked of women. You don't see men on panels, I have four partners in Cohen Reznik Capital, and you don't see them being asked this question. And I think it does a disservice to us on multiple levels. One, it implies that somehow, I am struggling in a way that they are not. That I am more committed to my family than my male counterparts or that I am somehow less committed to my job than my male partners. I think that's an unfair implication of asking this question of women repeatedly.

I think it also does [my male partners] a disservice in implying that they do not want to be with their families and that they're not having these exact same struggles or having to ... be efficient with their time because of the exact same thing.

I always find that question frustrating; it's usually a well-meaning young woman, who actually wants to know, so I don't really hold it against them for asking. But that question really frustrates me as a woman in finance and a manager of a bank.

As a father of two young girls (5 and 1 thank you for asking), this really spoke to me. Like many parents, there are times that I miss my kids and times where I need a break, which is the same for everyone, and that's okay. Honestly, it's a mixed bag when I take time away for any reason. Work travel is a particularly sensitive subject and one that women are scrutinized for much more than men. Von Ossen continued:

[Often] people are shocked that I travel for work and have this panicked expression of "Oh my gosh, did you just leave your 2 and

4-year-old at home on their own?" I see absolutely no difference between me [or], my male colleagues, doing that and yet there is this kind of judgment... and it's frustrating, it truly is.

Frankly, men and women are handling it the same way; it's support from partners and support through colleagues, and carving out what works for yourself. It's not easy, I'm by no means implying that I have this figured out. What I'm trying to propose is that this is the same for me as it is for my male colleagues and to imply otherwise is unfair to both of us.

Local Renewable Energy Associations

While the groups above are big national or international organizations, there are many other national, state, and local groups as well. Wikipedia lists forty-six such associations. They include:

- American Wind and Wildlife Institute
- Aprovecho (Cottage Grove, Oregon)
- Arizona Solar Center
- Biomass Thermal Energy Council
- Citizens for Responsible Energy Solutions
- Clean Power Now (Hyannis, MA)
- Energy Future Coalition
- Environmental and Energy Study Institute
- Geothermal Resources Council
- Global Energy Network Institute
- The Green Grid (Oregon)
- Interstate Renewable Energy Council (Latham, NY)
- Midwest Renewable Energy Association
- National Hydropower Association
- National Renewable Energy Laboratory (Golden, CO)

- National Solar Thermal Test Facility (Albuquerque, NM)
- North Carolina Solar Center
- Pacific Marine Energy Center
- Renewable Fuels Association (St. Louis, MO)
- Solar Cookers International (Sacramento, CA)
- Solar Energy Industries Association
- Solar San Antonio
- Yellowstone-Teton Clean Energy Coalition (Jackson, WY)
- And many more.[129]

Get to Know Your Ecosystem

In the renewable energy industry, there are additional organizations that support affiliated organizations and stakeholders. These could be trade associations, economic consortiums, unions, local chambers of commerce, or other nonprofits. Typically, these groups exist to foster new business and advocate on behalf of their members.

For local organizations, it's probably easiest to Google the territory along with a description of the group you're trying to find. Otherwise, links to local chapters of national organizations are typically listed on the national organization's website.

If you're just starting out, these are also great networking opportunities. Connect with the executive director or staff and share your story. Don't be afraid to ask questions—their job is to help! Some good inquiries include:

- Where and how often do you meet?
- If I'm just starting out, are there people or companies you'd encourage me to reach out to?

---

[129]https://en.wikipedia.org/wiki/Category:Renewable_energy_organizations_based_in_the_United_States

- Do you offer individual memberships?
- Are there scholarships for students or those with lower incomes?
- Do you have an emerging or young professionals group?

It's very important that you belong and contribute to these groups; the health of these organizations and the industry as a whole depends on the robustness of contributions from their members.

A few examples of how you can participate:

- Volunteer at an upcoming conference or meeting.
- Attend a happy hour or sponsored workshop.
- Offer to buy lunch for the executive director or staff member to pick their brain.

Go to an industry association chapter meeting, request a lunch networking date (expect to pay), and be visible. We all have some level of introversion, but understand that if you're genuine most people want to like you and see you succeed.

Lastly, if there are membership dues, and you can afford to join these groups, it's important to do so. If your goal is to influence policy or other decisions, usually there's a pay-to-play policy where having a vote is dependent on your support of the organization. Be generous with your time and other resources— it tends to come back in the form of good karma and new opportunities.

Following Through

After networking, do your best to follow through on *everything that you've committed to.* You don't want to be known as someone who drops the ball. We all get busy, of course, but even if it's a short email or text, make sure you show appreciation for people's time and efforts. That being said, be selective with your commitments.

If you've read Malcolm Gladwell's *Outliers*, then you may be familiar with special circumstances that create success. He provides many instances of being in the right place at the right time, and my experience in solar has been illustrative of that. As a technophile, budding marketer, and social media kid, basic oughts'-era skills helped my early development in the industry.

Born in the mid-80s, I spent too much of my youth on Nintendo and watching cartoon advertisements, too much of my adolescence in chat rooms and college-years on Facebook. Consequently, I was fluent in digital communication and marketing in my early career, which was critical to my success as the local clean energy economy evolved.

Also, germane to my professional maturation was the advent of Community Solar in Minnesota, my adopted home state. Community solar programs allow residents and organizations to participate in off-site solar farms, where credits materialize on their utility bills based on their level of participation in a particular project. Many people and businesses can't physically install solar panels on their roofs and community solar offers them an alternative. Consequently, projects became massive in size and the Minnesota market exploded from about 10 megawatts statewide in 2013 to roughly 1,000 megawatts (1 gigawatt) in 2020, 100 times larger. If our program had started anywhere else, would I or my company be as successful? The answer is very likely "no."

The key takeaway is most opportunities present themselves to those who are at the right place at the right time. Much of this is outside your control, but in order to have a seat at the table, you have to be ready!

In clean energy, much like any other industry, the hiring process is hard, awkward, and exhausting for both sides. It takes a lot of effort for employers to respond to job openings, especially in smaller businesses. Having been solicited hundreds of times from potential employees, and hiring dozens of people, the advice in the following chapter comprises the ingredients for a successful hiring process, but the recipe is something that will take time and be unique to you.

Networking Tips with Jake Rozmaryn

In my 2020 interview with Jake Rozmaryn we discussed the current state of networking in clean energy:

I do not think it's as easy today to get into cleantech as it was when I started a decade ago when nobody had experience. It's definitely more competitive today. That being said there are new sectors now, and there will continue to be new sectors. Sectors today have a lot of growing up and learning to do, so experience from other areas that are more advanced can be important.

There are ways to accelerate your career in the clean energy space and cleantech broadly.

One program that I've referred many people to in the past few years and have seen some really cool success stories is the NYU Clean Start Certificate Program.[130] It's essentially a boot camp for people from different professional backgrounds that want to get into cleantech. It gives attendees a crash course education and in the end, puts them in a capstone project with a cleantech company. The process gives them the basic knowledge required and a line item on their resume that can open their next door. It's a phenomenal program and hugely successful. If you're a little more established and looking to pivot it's one of the best things you can do.

If you're earlier in your career or if a boot camp is not in the cards there are so many meetup groups, clean energy trade associations, incubators, and accelerators. In the Midwest, Clean

---

[130] http://ufl.nyc/ourprograms/cleanstart

Energy Trust is a non-profit VC that invests in early-stage cleantech companies.[131] There are so many different spheres of influence that you can start to imbed yourself into, through events through their community forums Those are great places to start networking; see if there is an internship opening.

For instance, if you get an internship at American Wind Energy Association, you could leverage that experience to get a job with one of their member companies. If it's an internship at an investor incubator or accelerator, you can try to get a position with one of the accelerator companies that spin out. Really try to get something out of those spheres of influence; it's one of the best things you can do.

Because these industries attract people that would describe themselves as incredibly passionate you have an opportunity to showcase that passion online. Beef up your LinkedIn, Twitter, or other platforms with that content. Engage in the online communities. Write articles. Someone that wanted to work for Antenna knew that we were interested in the intersection of energy and blockchain and showed us a series of papers he had written on energy and blockchain. That was someone who wanted to get into data science and I've referred them to 10 jobs already. People in the industry are so motivated by passion that when they see a person who shares that passion and is trying to get involved, people will be more inclined to help.

---

[131] https://www.cleanenergytrust.org/

9. Trust the (Application) Process

As you identify career opportunities and make your applications for jobs, it's important that you're able to effectively *communicate* your skills and experience. After all, your prospective employer probably doesn't know you, and their first impression will be what they see on your resume and cover letter. If those look good, then the next impression they will form of you is at your first interview.

There are countless resources on crafting a resume, cover letter and interviewing. You can find them anywhere. In this book, I'll provide the most important set of do's and don'ts for the clean energy industry.

Your Resume and Cover Letter

Here are the five key points you must remember:

1.) If you don't have a resume, go online, and find a standard resume template. Use a format that's simple and informative. Do not attempt to "re-invent the wheel" by concocting your own innovative resume format. The employer wants to know that you can create a straightforward business document, and no one will be overly-impressed by your attempts at creativity. A resume is a ubiquitous business document that must be crystal clear and concise. If a hiring manager picks up your resume and spends more than ten seconds trying to understand it, he or she will move on. That being said, a resume should stand out visually. Take some time to add your personality (just don't use comic sans). You can find several simple, eye-catching examples at www.cleanwavebook.com/resources .

2.) Don't just provide a boring list of jobs you've held. Highlight your career accomplishments as a set of goals reached or problems solved. Include any examples where you increased sales, introduced a new solution, solved a problem, or saved the company money. No organization wants an employee who's content to merely punch the clock; they want someone who can help build the company.

3.) Never lie about your education or invent credits. Does it need elaboration? Once your reputation is tarnished there's not much you can do to mend it.

4.) If you're fresh out of college or high school and have little work history, that's okay if you're applying for the appropriate job. While your resume will be short, a prospective employer will be hiring you based on your interview and their assessment of your attitude and willingness to learn and be a team player. Make sure that your passion for clean energy is communicated clearly. For most jobs, your resume should fit on one page. For executive and highly technical positions, it can go to two pages.

5.) If sending a paper resume, never use scented stationery. Never send gifts. Keep your cover letter short and concise. Always double-check your spelling and grammar—one typo can kill your chances.

The Interview

Congratulations! Your resume passed the first screening and someone—the HR director, department hiring manager, or whoever will be supervising you—has asked for an interview. Here are eight bullet-proof tips for how to succeed in this important step.

1.) Research the company and what it does. Nothing turns off an interviewer more quickly than an applicant who appears to know nothing about the company. Go online and read the company's website and look at press coverage. Try to discern from the job description and other information any special projects or challenges the company is facing. When the interviewer asks if you're familiar with the company, you must be able to say, "Absolutely! What aspect of the organization do you want to discuss?"

2.) Observe all the normal rules of protocol. Arrive on time— not a minute late. Be properly dressed, and by that I mean wear the type of clothing that you would be expected to wear to work. It's possible to overdress for a job interview. If you're applying for a job in the call center, don't come to the interview wearing an expensive suit—you'll look weird and pretentious. For executives, you should go to the company's website and see if they have an "about us" page with bios and photos of the executive team. Dress the way they do. For example, if none of the men are wearing neckties, don't wear one. If the women are wearing sleeves, make sure you do the same.

It might go without saying but do not wear strong perfume or cologne. Unless you're applying for a job as a creative (and if you don't know what that means, then you're not), keep your overall appearance neat and collected. If you have a personal flair I say use it, but make sure it doesn't detract from your core message which is providing value to their organization.

3.) In the interview, act as though you already work for the person you're talking to. Your inner attitude should be not "Please give me the job" but "Here's how I can help you solve your problems and meet your goals." Make the person feel like you'd have things covered on day one. Don't be pushy, and be sure to listen carefully. You need to be a good team player and make your department look good in the eyes of your supervisor and team.

4.) You may be asked the usual interview questions such as "Name one mistake you've made" or "Where do you see yourself in five years?" Try not to be flustered by these annoying boilerplate queries; just give a quick, pleasant answer and then pivot by asking your own question about some aspect of the job.

5.) If your interviewer seems bored or asks only routine questions (see #4 above), or does not make eye contact, then you may not want to work for this company even if you're asked to come back for a second interview.

6.) If you possess specialized knowledge, especially from a previous job, it's possible that the interviewer has no intention of hiring you, but only wants to pick your brain. Be careful if he or she starts asking about solutions to specific problems. You'll have to play along, but don't be surprised if they don't hire you.

7.) Under no circumstances should you badmouth or criticize your previous employer. Even if your experience with your previous employer was horrible and, in your opinion, your boss was either totally incompetent or a jerk, keep it to yourself. If your interviewer asks why you left the company (and in fact, you left voluntarily—you were neither laid off nor fired), simply say that you felt you had made certain accomplishments and it was time to move on.

If you were fired, don't be bitter, but be honest and provide a brief explanation. If you were laid off, simply say so, and that it was a management decision to downsize.

8.) Many job coaches say that after the interview, you should send a thank-you email to the person or people who interviewed you. Personally, I think it's a solid idea. A hand-written note mailed to the interviewer(s) is best. If that's not possible, a unique email or e-card works too.

Here are a few more key pointers:

Be Prepared

Know with whom you're networking or interviewing. There's usually a lot of information available publicly; impress them with data or insight relevant to their field. But unless you want "stalker" scratched on your resume personal info should be left out (not applicable if you know their family, friends, or colleagues).

Proofread Your Application Materials

Know common grammar missteps and avoid them. Nothing is more annoying, to me at least, than someone typing "your" when it should be "you're" or "then" when it should be "than." To be certain you haven't missed anything, use automated software such as Grammarly.

Be Respectful

If someone has the decency to confirm a meeting or phone call, you'd better not be either late or too early. Commonly, this means showing up a minute or two before your meeting time. Also, if someone gives you a "hard no," it's not okay to press the issue; respect their response and move on.

Be Pleasantly Annoying

Making light of the hiring situation is by no means off-color. For example, one time someone sent me an email with the title "Don't Ghost Me Just Because It's Halloween," and another sent a daily recurring event invitation when I hadn't followed up with a deliverable. Let's be honest; the business world is usually very dry and boring. Spice it up with your own spin when working with others, it helps to make things less serious and more fun!

Didn't Get Hired? Move on to the Next Opportunity

If all of the above doesn't work, move on to the next opportunity quickly. Rejection is a natural and expected part of any business and in particular the competitive clean energy economy. Also, people are busy, so don't take it personally if there's not an immediate response to your inquiries.

Climbing Ladders

In 2007, fresh off my successful global tour I shocked the world by hanging up my guitar to look for a "real job." Obviously, I'm joking, there was a long rehab stint in between.[132] As alluded to earlier, I graduated in the fall of 2006, after a very distinguished five and a half years at the University of Minnesota.[133] That fall I started getting serious about looking for a job, mainly because I saw my short-term future and it didn't involve having money, and hence a girlfriend.

An Inconvenient Truth was a turning point for me and many others. Al Gore is still a hero of mine, and unfortunately, he continues to be a very polarizing figure. The documentary was the right message – urgent action is needed to address a devolving environmental catastrophe – but Gore was the wrong messenger. Coming from a Democrat in an era of diverging politics, no republican could embrace his message. If a moderate from the right like John McCain had carried the torch, would we be in a different place today? Hypotheses aside, those that embraced the science were appalled that we'd allowed the fossil fuel interests to walk away with our future. So, I started researching ways in which I could be part of the solution.

That fall I'd spent time finishing up my final online classes. With the maturity level of a college-age musician I'd smoke weed and hang out at the library pretty often, which was a recipe for a great but not very productive afternoon. One of my classes was an advanced English Literature course which was also one of my

---

[132] Kidding again, but addiction is no joke and I realize that. If you need help, seek it – no shame in getting help.

[133] My GPA was just slightly above disgusting.

favorites. Reading Yeats, Bronte, and Joyce is something everyone should have the pleasure of doing. My other course, funny enough, was a career prep class which was mildly helpful; apparently, there's a lot of intuitive advice for job searching (weird!).

In between daydreams, I'd also started to study for the GRE, opening the door for a potential MBA stint. One major takeaway for me was that there's definite value in learning. Vocab associations, critical writing, math, all useful skills that improved the effectiveness of how I communicate. Again, the thirst for knowledge is a gift that keeps on giving. In the end, once I'd started working, it became increasingly evident that taking time away from my passion and focus just wasn't in the cards.

In October of 2006, I'd started my job search in earnest. After discovering my "why," I channeled that motivation into finding work that would help me suplex the climate crisis into submission. During my research I discovered that several industries were experiencing high growth. Both solar and wind at that time were on a roughly 40% year over year growth curve, and both technologies fit the mold as carbon assassins.

Outside of renewable energy, I had a few interviews, including with an international shipping company. The more I thought about that opportunity the more I hated the idea of contributing to the substantial CO_2 pollution pervasive in the shipping industry.[134]

Resumés went out to dozens of different companies. All but one went unanswered. It was Innovative Power Systems Incorporated, in Minneapolis. A guy by the name of Jamie Borell messaged back that they might have an opening in sales, and I hated the idea of sales.

During the interview, I met with Jamie and the founder Ralph Jacobson, in a dingy basement of an old warehouse just north of

---

[134] According to Wikipedia the shipping industry emits 2.2% of worldwide human-caused CO_2.

the university. As mentioned earlier in the book, it was musky down there: likely mold, potentially the black plague, but there was also an understated excitement, which also could have been the severely garish orange walls adorning the conference room. In any case, the interview went relatively well, and despite the potential for respiratory problems I was convinced that this was my future.

Years later I had a Kaiser Soze-esque[135] moment. At the interview I'd noticed that Jamie's arm was in a sling, he'd fallen down a flight of stairs a week or two earlier. I understood later that likely one of the influencing factors in my hiring was to get someone else to scale ladders and measure roofs. In any case, the job seemed dangerous which added to the sex appeal.

For the month or so after my interview, I persistently followed up on a weekly basis, and finally, my start date was set for early January 2007. My first few weeks were spent diving into the technology, reading articles, and working on special projects. Answering phone calls was brutal as I struggled to make any coherent sense, but I faked it 'till I made it. Soon I was working on proposals, meeting with clients, and within five months I sold my first project – a two-panel solar hot water system for a young family in West St. Paul. I will always remember and appreciate those early clients who took a chance on solar in its relative infancy and took a chance on me in particular.

The other aspect of my early days that I appreciated, later on, was working on the install team. To supplement my income, which was 100% commission-based, I helped the crews install various residential and commercial solar projects. Quickly, I absorbed information related to attachment methods, high-level

---

[135] If you haven't seen Usual Suspects, do yourself a favor and go straight to Blockbuster. (Yes, I realize that at the time of this writing anything starring Kevin Spacey is not en vogue)

engineering, and other practical knowledge that helped me up the learning curve.

Everything was a struggle, however. The first year, my total income was below the poverty line. One of the only things that helped me take a leap of faith and stick with it was that I recently graduated from college and was an expert on cheap living. It was a small success though because the country was on the precipice of financial disaster. Surviving those early years set me up for significant growth later on.

10. Entrepreneurialism

"When it comes to marketing, creative resources are often worth far more than dollars."

–Neil Blumenthal, co-founder, and co-CEO of Warby Parker.

Addressing the climate crisis will inherently require new ideas, the creation of which will spawn new companies and new industries as outlined in previous chapters.

Entrepreneurship is a gift. In the best of times, it's one of the most rewarding things you can possibly do with your life. In the worst of times, well, it's not great. Entrepreneur's etymology is French and it means one who undertakes. It's a perfect descriptor, someone whose initiative is of their own volition. To undertake is to face things head-on.

As you've read, the primary goal of clean technology is to disrupt the status quo. It's not retreading the same water expecting different results; it's undertaking new ideas to change the way the world operates for the better. Entrepreneurs are a necessary part of this revolution because their ideas are driving innovation and creating the future.

Entrepreneurship with Jake Rozmaryn

Optimism

At the highest level, cleantech professionals are trying to change the status quo. They're changing infrastructure which is inherently hard; it's not a consumer widget that you can bring to market in 3 months. Its systemic change. You can only try to do the impossible if you have an undeniable drive, are a self-starter, and super-passionate about what you're doing because the nature of what you're doing is seemingly impossible.

You have to be able to trust the people around you and trust that they can advance the mission because you'll never be able to do it all yourself. One of my biggest regrets getting started was that I never had a partner that was invested at the level that I was as a founder. I will start more businesses no doubt but never as a sole founder. It's such a hard thing to do. It helps to do it with someone to share that burden, to have someone you can be comfortable with to share the ups and downs.

Entrepreneurship

Entrepreneurship to me means looking for lines. When you go to the grocery store and you see a long line of people; that's a pain point - people don't want to be there. What's the solution? Self-checkout, checkout in advance on an app, buy-online, home delivery, pickup window. Take that analogy, there are lines everywhere.

Three or four years ago there were battery systems coming out and we needed to make sure they worked with solar. Now there are these companies selling software to optimize solar and storage. That was a line that people observed and came up with great solutions. Those opportunities exist everywhere. Look at unsustainable fishing practices and plastic in the oceans; those are lines where a million solutions need to be developed and come to life. If you have an open mind and appreciate that opportunities and challenges are everywhere you can will a lot of things into existence because the problems exist. We need as many people as possible to address them.

There's so much work to be done. There's so, so much work to be done. Opportunities are everywhere. Solar has become boring, but the fact that solar is boring is a good thing. It means it's been commoditized! It's mainstream. We need all of cleantech to be boring. There's an unlimited number of things that are not boring and that means there are opportunities everywhere.

Idea Sex

Author and entrepreneur James Altucher coined the term Idea Sex, which is a thesis that taking an effective concept from one space, and transposing it to another may, if done correctly, result in novel success. Nico Johnson outlined an example of this:

In clean energy, Jigar Shah worked for BP, one of the biggest wind manufacturers in the world, and saw that developers were using a mechanism called the Power Purchase Agreement[136] and thought, wow, maybe this could unlock solar as a financeable asset. We all know the benefits and opportunities that it created.[137] He went on to start SunEdison which became the largest and most influential distributed solar development company in the world,

[136] The Power Purchase Agreement (PPA's) has been the single most disruptive business tool in US solar energy. It unlocked significant capital and project deployment in the scale of gigawatts. With substantial tax incentives available to projects, PPA's allowed for the efficient monetization of those credits (vital for non-tax-paying entities like schools and non-profits), and developers were able offer no-upfront cost financing. An entire book could be devoted solely to the PPA, but this brief background should give you a very basic understanding of what you need to know.

[137] Commercial and residential PPA's have unlocked gigawatts of solar development in the US.

with much of that success owed to his experience at BP. It goes back to the ability to transfer knowledge from one industry to another.

This was also true for John Novak, founder, and CEO of Scanifly; a drone-based solar site evaluation and design tool. Novak worked for several well-known east-coast solar firms before stopping out to start his venture. He had a background in landscape architecture which made him a good fit for project design, working on site analyses where he measured roofs and identified tree species along with their estimated future heights (important for shade analysis). John noted how long and arduous the design process would take, and oftentimes how inaccurate the results were.

He tinkered behind the scenes, off-hours, building a drone, and experimenting with various tools. Drone technology improved and became commonplace in other commercial spaces like roofing. It made sense to build a software solution to help solar companies improve their processes. Novak saw how transformative the technology was elsewhere and adapted it to serve the solar market.

International Business with Nico Johnson

Opening a new international market is no different than starting a new business. It's always going to take twice as long and cost twice as much as you had thought when you started.

It's amazing how many times I run into examples of when companies tried to stick to their guns instead of budgeting twice as much as they thought they needed. They hired small.

I had a lot of friends who have come in and out of the industry in Latin America, who didn't realize as I didn't in 2013, how hyper-local all of these markets are, and how dependent they are on other fuel sources. If you're developing solar in Europe and the

US, natural gas and coal are big drivers in those electricity markets and you have to understand how they move pricing in order to be effective.

I remember Daniel [Ades] the CEO of Kawa and I were looking at investing in a 125-megawatt Panamanian solar portfolio[138]. We paid $20,000 for an independent entity to provide a forecast of what the country's energy matrix would look like over the next 5-7 years. Their analysis concluded that it was likely oil would settle at $50 a barrel, which would make the projects unprofitable. [Daniel] said, "your spreadsheet looks perfect and this project definitely looks like it's penciling, however, the thing that scares me is that *if* $50 is the new normal, then we'll be betting against a 100-year-old industry and I'm not willing to do that."

Over the next 18 months oil stabilized around $50 a barrel, natural gas started to take off, and all of our projections about natural gas were below what they turned out to be.

There were all of these external factors affecting the market price and it reminds me of trying to launch a start-up. There are so many external factors that can change overnight to impact the profitability of a previously profitable idea, that you have no control over. If you don't know they exist it's very, very difficult to thrive.

Across the entire spectrum, it requires a tribute of specialists. In international business most importantly, the companies I saw fail most often and failed the fastest were companies that were unwilling to hire local early. There's a huge opportunity for someone in automotive or telecom, or even working at a big marketing firm, to transition to clean energy as *the* local expert. At Trina, I was the sole representative. I spoke fluent Spanish but I didn't get the traction that Jinko did when they hired two local sales guys who immediately took over the market.

---

[138] The cost of a portfolio like this in 2015 would have probably exceeded $200 million USD.

My advice to job-seekers in Latin America: become good at understanding your market and sell that specialty and expertise. Trina and Conergy were unwilling to hire a local partner or person that knew the end market early enough. As a company, you can go to China and speak perfect Mandarin, but if you walk into a business meeting with a CEO you better make damn sure you have an interpreter. From a company's standpoint, don't have the hubris to think you know the market well enough.

So, from that perspective, if I were to do it all over again, I probably would have followed some of my colleagues who went to some of these bigger players like Soler Direct (who were bought by EDF) and Sunetics (former AES employees). You can draw a line back, at almost every turn, from successful solar development and asset ownership companies to the utility power industry. It all feeds back to this idea that if you don't understand the macro-scale, you'll never be an executioner at the micro.

Starting a Business with Jigar Shah

In a 2019 interview with the Sounds of Solar podcast[139] Jigar Shah shared some insight into starting businesses in clean energy:

You learn early on that going to consumers and asking them to pay for 7 – 8 years of energy upfront to buy a solar energy system will lose a lot of customers. Typical responses are: "I really want to get solar, but I need to send my kid to summer camp, I need to redo my kitchen. My car is on its last leg." You get dropped down the priority list. There needed to be a dedicated way for people to say yes, and that is how solar as a service was born. If you go to people

---

[139] https://www.evs-eng.com/sounds-solar/

and say, just pay for what you use, then they weren't comparing the purchase to other things in their life.

There are a lot of things that have gotten easier. How to work with a law firm. How to work with an accounting firm. How to work with finance companies. All that stuff you learn along the way, but when I think about what served me well, it's just treating people with respect. It's extraordinary to me how many people treat some people better than others. This industry is very small. There's only like 5,000 – 10,000 professionals that move around and become director of engineering here or CEO there. If you piss everybody off along the way then you won't really have anybody to work with. I'm naturally somebody who has a lot of respect for other people and that has served me well.

When I started Sun Edison, we were selling to Walmart, and Target, Staples, and Wholefoods but the profit margins we were making were really high. I built Sun Edison with a $97,000 home equity loan and $20,000 worth of savings for almost two and a half years. So it's incredible to me how people now raise $5 million, burn through it all, and have nothing to show for it. And they ask for another $5 million to make it to the other side. No, you're just terrible at business and should just shut down.

It's about finding a niche where you think your expertise and a little bit of capital can unlock something. Whatever it is you want to go after you need to be able to double or triple that money. Otherwise, there's no reason to start a company.

Green Island

After college, I grew closer to my Dad and his side of the family. Traveling to Hawaii felt like a homecoming every time I'd make the trip; barbeques with cousins, aunts, and uncles. In 2012, coinciding with declining business and incentives in Minnesota I'd started to think about developing solar in Hawaii. Most of my family there were electricians, pretty convenient for creating a solar side-business.

My dad and I playing some ukuleles

I formed an LLC called Green Island and took trips every few months; reaching out to Hawaiian partners and potential clients in the evenings from my home in the Midwest. It was fun to start something new and my dad was more excited than I was. We'd have regular phone conversations about the technology and opportunities. He'd worked over 30 years in commercial lighting at the Polynesian Cultural Center on the north shore of Oahu. You could tell that he wanted more, and the idea of solar business gave him a needed reprieve from daily life.

We pitched several dozen businesses and homeowners but had little uptake. After about 18 months of trying I'd decided to refocus on Minnesota as solar policies improved there. I'd failed to gain traction working both in Minnesota and Hawaii, but learned a lot about myself and my dad. I also learned that in order to be successful in something you really need to be 100% committed to it. The lone projects that got to the finish line were a few rooftop installations for condo associations on the Big Island.

My dad passed away in 2015 of heart disease and unfortunately never got the satisfaction of seeing those systems installed. But I'm grateful for that time we had together.

Solar project I helped to develop near Kona, HI

11. Marketing Yourself and Your Ideas

"When it comes to marketing, creative resources are often worth far more than dollars."

- Neil Blumenthal, co-founder, and co-CEO of Warby Parker.

"You don't need a corporation or a marketing company to brand you now: you can do it yourself. You can establish who you are with a social media following."
- Ray Allen, American former professional basketball player.

"You have to understand your own personal DNA. Don't do things because I do them or Steve Jobs or Mark Cuban tried it. You need to know your personal brand and stay true to it."

-Gary Vaynerchuk

In today's markets, it's more important than ever that you're part of the conversation. The goal is to cast yourself as an authority in whichever field you focus on. There are many ways to promote yourself and your ideas, but it's essential to do so while maintaining decorum.

Leadership

As I discussed in the previous chapter, most industries have representative groups and stakeholder organizations that advocate on behalf of their interests. Get to know them, volunteer, and run for leadership positions. Participants are typically leaders who can help you with informal mentorship or even internship or career opportunities. Take these people out to lunch or a drink, with the goal of gaining perspective on a particular issue or some other benign motive. If they're super busy (and most people are these days), then find out if there's an upcoming conference or industry happy hour they'll be attending where you can grab a few minutes. A page straight from Networking 101.

In 2019, I started searching for leadership opportunities within the industry and have joined the boards of Minnesota Solar Energy Industry Association and local non-profit advocacy organization Fresh Energy. As the Clean Energy movement grows, so must our individual commitments to help foster it. Standing behind these groups, influencing their next phases of operation, is extremely important. Those efforts will reverberate beyond near-term wins to provide stability and space for future success.

Social Media

Fortunately, and unfortunately, there is not a more critical platform for ideas than the internet and specifically social media. For professional settings, LinkedIn and Twitter are best. Make sure that your profiles are up to date with quality photos and positive messaging. Your posts should be free of insensitive or off-color content and instead focus on your passions and professional interests. There are plenty of good resources to help you in this space; below are a few suggestions if you're getting started or need a social media tune-up:

1) Share your passions. Use your social media as a tool for expressing your interests.

2) Polish your posts. Don't post thoughtlessly. Make your characters count, both on and off Twitter.

3) Tailor your talk. Before you post, craft messaging to create a positive impact on your desired audience.

4) Don't be afraid to connect. Use social media as a tool to reach out to people directly.

5) Get engaged. Be an active participant on social media by commenting and sharing your expertise.

Personal Branding

Besides your social media presence, you should have a personal website or blog. If your name is available as a domain (e.g., ericpasi.com), pick it up for cheap and plant an inexpensive and simple landing page or website as a hub for content. If it isn't, find some tangential domain and put a stake in the ground. As your online references grow, it enhances your search engine optimization (SEO) and generates (hopefully) positive results when anyone searches your name online.

If you are self-employed, make sure you have a professional-looking business card and website. These days you can hire a graphic designer and web designer to do this work on your behalf for between $500 to $1,000, and a recurring $50-$100 per year in hosting. This will be money well invested if you're committed to your future in the industry. Even if you're unemployed, many sites like Vistaprint, Moo, and others have great-looking stationery templates that are free and can deliver business cards for as little as $20.

Persuasion

Creating influence within your circles requires you to read people, react, and persuade them to your point of view. It is the root of sales and politics, and unfortunately (or fortunately, depending on how you look at it), the business world revolves around your ability to do both well.

One of the best business books ever written is *How to Win Friends and Influence People* by Dale Carnegie, and I recommend everyone read it. It offers a plethora of simple, time-tested, and valuable anecdotes about how to conduct yourself in professional settings. It's a model for pretty much everyone to become a better listener, communicator, and colleague.

Bending people's perceptions is an art form that is built over time. Like any other skill, it requires both practice and patience. Big or innately complex organizations like Fortune 500s and large municipalities are difficult to penetrate because you're not only competing with your ability to express ideas, but you're also competing with everyone else within that organization, whose members could number in the tens of thousands.

Understanding this was a key reason for me choosing to start at a smaller company, and why I suggest that everyone gains exposure in entrepreneurial settings. Your impact on day-to-day operations is so much bigger and you gain real-life experience in many aspects of the organization. Your decisions become more critical, you feel more involved, and that's exciting.

Once you've begun to hone your skills, it's important to put them to work. Be vocal, be persistent, be respectful, but above all else be *present* in the conversations that matter. If you aren't, your voice will be marginalized and you'll get less of what you want, and obviously, that's not a good thing. Persuasion is essentially the ability to sell ideas.

Leaders Are Learners

Education is a lifelong endeavor, period. Learning should not stop after high school or college. Continuous improvement is vital to not just staying ahead but keeping up. As time goes on, fresh talent will enter the workforce with new proficiencies, and existing contemporaries will pick up new competencies. By sitting on the sidelines, you're consigning yourself to obsolescence, so you might as well lead by learning. Remember my message from the previous chapter? The thirst for knowledge is a gift that keeps on giving.

Learning doesn't necessarily mean getting your MBA or reading a shelf-full of books every year (the latter would obviously help—the former is not for everyone). Erudition can take many forms. A few popular sources for information in clean energy are podcasts and email newsletters.

Podcasts are revolutionizing journalism and the dissemination of media. A podcast is an episodic series of digital audio or video files that a user can download and listen to at a time of their choosing. By allowing people to consume content at their convenience, podcasts are current, typically free, and specific to whatever topic you're interested in. Whether you are commuting, working out, traveling, cooking, or just hanging out, there's almost always an opportunity to listen and learn.

Clean energy has several very influential podcasts. For solar, Suncast is extremely insightful most episodes include interviews with luminaries like Jigar Shah and Daniel Shugar. Greentech Media plays host to several podcasts including The Interchange which dives into different topics related to clean energy, and the Energy Gang, with the aforementioned Shah, Katherine Hamilton, and Stephen Lacey.

Email newsletters are also an easy and typically digestible way to stay up to speed. For nearly any market there are content creators and aggregators, which help to compile essential news of the day, week, or month. Local business and real estate newsletters from groups like bizjournals.com are helpful in keeping tabs on certain geographic areas. Yann Brandt's "SolarWakeUp" is very influential in the solar space.

Grassroots Advocacy Works!

In 2013, I worked for a campaign to pass what would be the most important solar legislation in Minnesota history. The Solar Jobs Act set forth a mandate for utilities to have 1.5% of their energy supply come from solar by 2020. This modest level would pave the way for nearly $2 billion[140] in investments, which were realized by mid-2019.

The most impactful part of the bill allowed for Xcel's Community Solar Gardens program. Groups like the aforementioned Fresh Energy and Minnesota Solar Energy Industry Association were critical in negotiating the bill's language and working with legislators in various committees. I even visited lawmakers at the capitol to advocate on behalf of the bill.

At that time I was volunteering with the Sierra Club, showing up evenings and Saturdays to phone bank. Free pizza and coffee were compensation for the dozens of hours spent dialing to connect people with their legislators, helping to galvanize

---

[140] 1.5% represented a little more than 1 gigawatt of solar, and estimating a build plus development cost of about $2.00 per Watt.

support. I even canvassed people outside local showings of *Chasing Ice,* a fantastic, if not horrifying, documentary about vanishing glaciers (well worth watching!). Afterall, that was our target demographic.

I'm not sure that any of those actions made a definitive difference, but what I am sure of is that everything helps. Grassroots organizing can make a dent in the future, and that's exactly what happened. On a cool, inauspicious day that May, the realization of so many  people's efforts became reality as Governor Dayton signed our bill to tempered fanfare.

Fast cut through six years and badda-bing badda-boom: IPS has helped to develop more than $300 million in solar projects as a direct result of that bill, all while becoming one of the most successful solar companies in the country. Advocacy matters!

Sales People Suck

At least that's what I thought in 2007 at the outset of my career. Money grubbing, faux-alphas, out to suck money from unsophisticated victims. Looking back, I wasn't totally wrong— there are salesmen and women out there scamming unwitting victims all the time. But it took me a while to get out of that mentality, especially when the only position available to me at the outset was sales. I had to learn to swim with no background or any clue as to what I was doing.

Nearly everyone is a salesperson. You're constantly selling yourself and your ideas regardless of title. Persuasion is a gift that can open horizons and change your life, and passion is the engine that churns. In my opinion, you can't be too passionate. As one of the most distinguished sales leaders in history Zig Ziglar once said, "For every sale you miss because you're too enthusiastic, you will miss a hundred because you're not enthusiastic enough."

That's the thing, though: you don't really need to know a lot in sales. Don't tell everybody, but you only really need passion (as evidenced in previous chapters), decorum (don't piss people off), and basic communication skills. Sales means helping people, at least that's what it means to me now.

Persistence, and the Five Types of Consumers

It goes without saying that persistence is critical when persuading people to your point of view. The beautiful thing about clean energy is that it's a growing industry with a bright future and that virtually anyone who owns a house or building can—and should—be a customer. But we know that the world of consumers is divided into five groups, and they need to be treated differently. This classification was introduced by Everett Rogers, a professor of communication studies, in his book *Diffusion of Innovations*, first published in 1962, and is now in its fifth edition (2003).

The five classifications of consumers are:

1.) Innovators are the first individuals to adopt an innovation. They are the youngest in age, willing to take risks, are very social, and have closest contact to scientific sources and interaction with other innovators. The innovator is the very first person in their group to buy an electric car or have solar panels installed on their roof. They are likely to see a new innovation and seek out how they can buy it—no sales pitch necessary!

2.) Early adopters form the second fastest category of individuals who adopt an innovation. Also, typically younger in age, with a higher social status, financial lucidity, and advanced education, these individuals have the highest degree of opinion leadership among the other adopter categories. These are the people who will buy an electric car after seeing a few of them in the neighborhood. As of 2020, in the United States, this group is showing a willingness to consider buying an electric car. Sales of plug-in passenger cars achieved a 2.5% market share of new car sales in 2019, up from 0.86% in 2016.[141]

3.) Early majority consumers will adopt an innovation after a longer length of time than the innovators and early adopters. They tend to have above-average social status, some contact with early adopters, but seldom hold positions of opinion leadership in a community. They'll buy an electric car after reading all the reviews and becoming convinced the product is reliable and a good investment.

4.) Late majority individuals are typically skeptical about any innovation, have below-average social status, very little financial lucidity, and very little opinion leadership. They may feel personally threatened by an innovation until it's been around so

---

[141] https://en.wikipedia.org/wiki/Electric_car_use_by_country

long that it's no longer an innovation. They will buy an electric car when there are so many of them on the road that they have become ubiquitous. Bloomberg New Energy Finance predicts that by 2040, electric cars could make up 57 percent—a majority—of all passenger car sales worldwide.[142]

5.) Laggards actively resist anything new and will adopt an innovation only long after it has ceased to be an innovation. Individuals in this category typically have an aversion to change, and are advanced in age, and show little to no opinion leadership. They tend to be focused on upholding a belief in tradition and have low social status and low financial fluidity. They will buy an electric car when they have no other choice.

If you are involved in marketing or sales, you'll need to know how to deal with these types of consumers. Remember, in an industry that offers an innovative product, the late majority person who says "no" today might say "yes" a year from now. Be the friend who is waiting to help them, and they'll come back when they're ready.

---

[142] https://www.cnn.com/2019/05/15/business/electric-car-outlook-bloomberg/index.html

Personal Branding with Jake Rozmaryn

Personal branding is so important today. What advice would you give to someone starting out fresh?

It all comes down to messaging. Whether we're working on a digital campaign or PR, our primary question is - what do you want your public voice to be? Once you figure that out, disseminating it in a way that's authentic, accessible, and credible is extremely important.

People respond to authenticity. When people hire someone to take over their social media and all of the sudden things sound like they're being written by a computer, you're not going to have the same impact.

In the advertising world, they talk about ad blindness[143] - regardless of platform (TV, print, radio, online) you've learned when and where the ads are so your eyes and ears can ignore them. Most marketing firms count an impression even though most of the time the viewer, reader, listener doesn't register it. We've conditioned ourselves to have that blindness. In the social media, world having a corporate handle, a corporate Twitter or LinkedIn account, to many is comparable to an advertisement they're blind to. So even if you're generating great content it'll still be subject to that same blindness because too often it's missing that personal authenticity you get from a human.

---

[143] Ad blindness, also known as banner blindness or banner noise is where visitors to a website consciously or subconsciously ignore banner-like information. This issue of ad blindness has developed into a topic of discussion for online publishers who have seen their online advertising revenue decline because their ads become 'invisible' to their users over time. (https://www.ezoic.com/what-is-ad-blindness/)

For every bit of effort that Antenna puts into a corporate LinkedIn, we're going to expect the executive team (with us helping in many cases) to participate on LinkedIn at the same level because people usually respond more to personal content than an organization's primary channel.

Credibility is built in a few ways. First off, consistency is huge. No one pays attention to the social media person that never posts anything and then all of a sudden likes 100 things and posts ten times in one day. For most people, this means once a day, for others it means much more or much less. The key is to remain as consistent as possible to whatever that commitment might be. Secondly, you should try to engage when and where it makes sense. Be relevant to your persona and brand.

In terms of accessibility, you want to be a resource. People don't like getting pitched which decreases your accessibility. You want to focus on offering value first and foremost. Your content should be used to inform, build on ideas, and share breaking news that's of interest to your ecosystem. Share important content and add a quick take that's no more than a few sentences to show you're engaged. That's going to be much more meaningful, and it doesn't need to be a huge time commitment like writing a blog three times a week.

There are quick ways to be authentic, credible, and accessible; the internet allows you to convey your messaging in real-time which is a powerful tool. Together all of your content should be curated in a way that captures the voice you're trying to convey.

Reaching out cold to potential clients, mentors, employers who get inundated all the time is often futile. What are some strategies that you've seen be successful?

Personalization is huge. When people write to me, my response rate is going to be much higher. Don't go on a rambling 15-paragraph thesis - get to the point. Be sure that you're really writing to the person, and that you understand who they are. Articulate why their insight is needed and think of some way to offer value as part of that conversation.

There are different ways of providing value. Early in my career when I'd try reaching out to people, they wouldn't take my meeting. But I learned quickly. To add value, I'd let them know I was writing an article to publish in TechCrunch and would love to get their perspective. Typically, I'd get a response in 5 minutes.

Earlier on in my career, I was helping to curate the Midwest Solar Expo and would offer the stage to someone, which was a great way to open the door. It's a really good platform - offering value without pitching someone. Figure out how to add value, no matter how small of a gesture it might be. "Hi, I saw this event and thought you might be interested - maybe I'll see you there." It could be the smallest of things but show that you're writing to me for a reason and you understand who I am. Tailor your email to how my insight could help specifically and put something on my radar that maybe I wasn't aware of. That's interesting.

What does the future of cleantech and branding look like and how might that differ from traditional advertising/marketing?

Historically, this has been one of the scrappiest industries, and one that has put the least amount of emphasis on traditional branding. There are a variety of reasons: they don't have the resources, their margins are super thin, they're still growing their business. It was incredibly amateur for a very long time. When I started my business EcoBrandit eleven years ago I wanted to help small solar installers with their digital presence and their marketing to compete with the Solar City's of the world. No one had less money on earth than a small residential solar installer. No one had less money than that guy.

These industries have become so much more mature, you've seen the booms and busts. You've seen scrappiness. You've seen the Solar Cities of the world spend $5,000 on customer acquisition just to sell a $20,000 solar system, and fail. You've seen the extremes. As companies become more mature their marketing, communications and branding will get more sophisticated. It's going to be more data-driven because everything will be about margin. As industries commoditize and organizations are squeezed in different ways, customer acquisition costs have to go down. Marketing has to get smarter.

Similar to what you've seen elsewhere, there are macro marketing trends toward the following:

- *Marketing automation*
- *Personalization*
- *Better customer support*
- *Visual story-telling*
- *Buy-at-your-own-pace*

Earlier in my career, it was clear that clean energy sectors had not advanced because of sustainability alone, they had advanced based on economics and financial return. After disasters like Hurricane Sandy in the Northeast, Camp Fire[144] in the Bay Area, and Covid19 globally, messaging has shifted slightly toward resiliency. Communication will continue to evolve. Sustainability messaging has never been most prominent but that's not to say it won't be. Climate, sustainability, environment, clean energy, cleantech – all are more en vogue today than they've ever been. If ten years ago

---

[144] The Camp Fire will be one of those defining moments for clean energy. PG&E's bankruptcy aside, the fact that planned outages have become commonplace as a forest fire prevention strategy is a turning point for communities and individuals to start thinking critically about resilience.

someone would have told me that solar will be the hottest thing you could do in 2020, I would've said "oh that'd be nice." Times have changed.

How do you use data, personalization, automation to educate people efficiently about these technologies and convert them into customers? The sloppiness of the Solar City days are over. The era of big data and leveraging technology to make things more efficient has begun.

12. Having Fun

Congratulations to your future self (hopefully!), you've found a pathway into one of the most dynamic and satisfying industries in the world. This is no time to rest on those laurels, though. Buckle up and kick it into insane mode – this going to be a wild ride. But now that you're here, what's next?

Hustle & Flow

No, not the underrated mid-aughts rap movie featuring Ludacris - Hustle and Flow is a high-level concept where monumental effort (Hustle) results in a state of heightened productivity (Flow). Once you've found your place in the world it's time to put your head down and get to work.

As alluded to earlier in the book, nothing worth substance will be handed to you. Clean energy, similar to tech in general, rewards colossal effort. Love or hate him, Tesla founder Elon Musk is the undeniable personification of Hustle. A 2018 article published by Recode[145] reported first-hand accountings from his colleagues that Musk was "working 120 hours per week while 'everyone' at Tesla worked 100 hours per week at times that year as Tesla ramped up production of its Model 3 sedan. He suggested the long hours were necessary for Tesla to survive."

While it might sound like hyperbole, that type of behavior has been substantiated by many who have worked with him.[146] Greatness typically requires bold action and Musk excels in both categories. The markets have rewarded Tesla for its employee's blood and sweat by crowning it America's most valuable auto manufacturer, ahead of Ford, GM, and Chrysler. The 120-hour workweek is not necessary to succeed in cleantech, but being a "hustler" can help new entrants reach farther, faster.

The *flow state* was originally a term coined by psychologist Mihály Csíkszentmihályi, in his 1990 book titled simply *Flow.* According to Csíkszentmihályi, *flow* is defined as an "optimal state of consciousness where we feel our best and perform our best." It involves "being completely involved in an activity for its own sake. The ego falls away. Time flies. Every action, movement, and thought follows inevitably from the previous one, like playing jazz. Your whole being is involved, and you're using your skills to the utmost."

---

[145] https://www.vox.com/2018/11/2/18053428/recode-decode-full-podcast-transcript-elon-musk-tesla-spacex-boring-company-kara-swisher
[146] https://www.businessinsider.com/ex-tesla-employees-reveal-the-worst-parts-of-working-there-2019-9#the-long-hours-4

Fellow psychologist and author Owen Schaffer further refined the conditions that define flow in 2013[147] as:

- Knowing what to do
- Knowing how to do it
- Knowing how well you are doing
- Knowing where to go (if navigation is involved)
- High perceived challenges
- High perceived skills
- Freedom from distractions

Schaffer further defined the flow sensation from interviews with individuals who have 'experienced' it firsthand:

- Completely involved in what we are doing – focused, concentrated.
- A sense of ecstasy – of being outside everyday reality.
- Great inner clarity – knowing what needs to be done, and how well we are doing.
- Knowing that the activity is doable – that our skills are adequate to the task.
- A sense of serenity – no worries about oneself, and a feeling of growing beyond the boundaries of the ego.
- Timelessness – thoroughly focused on the present, hours seem to pass by the minute.
- Intrinsic motivation – whatever produces flow becomes its own reward.

When you can grind away in an environment that's rewarding, and realize the fruits of your labor, it feels less work-like and more

---

[147] http://humanfactors.com/whitepapers/crafting_fun_ux.asp

personally gratifying. Cheers to us all finding our own "flow" in whatever form that takes.

Avoid the Noise

Stay above the fray when it comes to gossip or triviality. In your career, stay focused on your purpose and your work. Needless to say, it's counterproductive to be caught in a cycle that isn't focused on your goals and well-being. Keep your head down and stay the course.

In a 2017 article by in Psychology Today titled *The Comparison Trap,*[148] author Rebecca Webber remarked that "measuring the self against others is a modus operandi of the human mind, and in some ways, it can be helpful. The inspiration you feel about someone else's achievements can rev up the motivation to improve your own life. The recognition that your abilities are a notch above someone else's can deliver a boost to your self-esteem. But comparisons can be harmful when they leave you feeling chronically inferior or depressed."

It's easy to get distracted by the one-upmanship that's so prevalent in western society. Social connectedness has only exacerbated this problem. We can all get wrapped up in the façade of other people's success. In clean energy, it's common to see acquisitions, mergers, ribbon- cuttings, and press releases. It can be a real distraction from your productivity, and not worth obsessing about. Instead, channel your energy into addressing the things that got you started in the space, to begin with. Maybe that's helping people, fighting the climate crisis, or immersing yourself into the technology. Whatever it is, be humble, be thankful, and look on the bright side.

---

[148] https://www.psychologytoday.com/us/articles/201711/the-comparison-trap

Physical and Mental Health

Physical *and* mental health are paramount to high performance. The consistent up-and-down market nature of clean energy paired with the rapid improvement of technology creates a tension that's somewhat unique. You've got to take care of yourself if you're going to have longevity in any industry, but particularly here.

Make sure your calendar allows for some form of physical activity several times per week. There are countless resources available for people who need help in jump-starting their physical well-being. Keep in mind that your employer may offer free or reduced-cost gym memberships – take advantage of it! Your office, apartment, or home may have workout equipment – don't waste those opportunities. Get up early, squeeze exercise in after work, or during lunch, be creative in scheduling the time.

Although physical health has been in the spotlight for decades, mental health is finally getting it's due. The truth is that physical and mental health go hand-in-hand and both must be present for true wellness. But this isn't news to most. In an interview at 'Great Place to Work For All' Summit and subsequent article at greatplacetowork.com,[149] Dr. Jeffrey Pfeffer of Stanford University shared his viewpoint on wellness in the workplace.

Dr. Jeffrey is an expert in workplace health whose research primarily focuses on the effects of work environments on human health and well-being. The article estimates that unhealthy work environments cost society a staggering $130 billion and 125,000 deaths each year. Employers are starting to put a larger emphasis on their employees' health, which is obviously a trend that's good for both sides.

---

[149] https://www.greatplacetowork.com/resources/blog/the-top-7-workplace-factors-that-impact-employee-health

As much as Musk's 120-hour workweek can be glorified in the media and popular culture, balance is obviously important. A study of about 5,000 people found that performance is not positively correlated to work hours. The findings, which were published in Morten Hansen's book *Great at Work*, showed that more hours worked intuitively led to lower productivity per hour worked. What Musk and other detractors may point to is that you can make up for inefficiency with volume – but at what cost? The age-old trope of working smarter not harder is legit. From the Great Place to Work article:

According to Dr. Pfeffer, long work hours 'are associated with adverse health, including cardiovascular disease, diabetes, disability.' Employers need to acknowledge this fact and encourage workers to leave after their workday is done to enjoy time with family and friends, without the stigma often associated with 'leaving early.'

For office workers, sitting (or standing) endlessly behind screens may help reach near-term goals. Those engaged in the field may also find that those long hours correlate to healthy paychecks. The toll of long hours can weigh heavily on personal relationships. The Great Place to Work article continued:

Pfeffer's research shows that social support—family and friends you can count on, as well as close relationships—can have a direct effect on health and buffers the effects of various psychosocial stresses, including workplace stress, that can compromise health.

Many people have to make hard trade-offs every day about work and family commitments. School talent shows should be enjoyed by all parents, not just those that stay home. You shouldn't have to feel guilty for taking your child or aging parent to the doctor, yet for many people, these events are stress-producing because they feel they are always letting down either their family or their manager/team.

There are a myriad of digital resources for individuals to address this topic. A 2018 article[150] by 24Seven Talent emphasized the importance of these issues to the health to your career while providing some helpful tips:

Take a break – *if you've just finished a difficult conversation with a customer or coworker, get up and walk outside for a few minutes. A change of scenery and a break will help you feel like facing the next battle.*

Get enough sleep – *you'll feel better prepared mentally and less cranky regardless of what the day brings if you get enough rest at night.*

Eat a good breakfast – *your body and your mind need fuel for the day, and a healthy breakfast can give you the right start.*

Exercise regularly – *it not only improves your physical health, but it also releases endorphins that put you in a better state of mind.*

Talk to someone – *when you're feeling stressed, talk to someone about the situation. Many times, just talking can help you feel better and realize things aren't as bad as they seemed at first.*

Reward yourself – *don't be afraid to give yourself a special treat after a hard day at work. It will make things easier the next time you have something difficult to deal with.*

---

[150] https://www.24seventalent.com/blog/2018/01/03/how-important-physical-and-mental-health-are-to-your-career/

Enjoy life outside of work – *when you have fun activities to focus on in the evenings and weekends, it gives you something to think about when the workdays are long.*

The bottom line? Never compromise between your work and personal life. In your career, there will always be more to do, another job to complete – don't sacrifice the truly important things, like health and family, for transient accomplishments.

Defining What Really Matters – Amanda Bybee

It's important to keep perspective. Much like the rest of the business world, clean energy is full of highs and lows, wins, and losses. The photovoltaic industry affectionately refers to this constant ebb and flow as the Solarcoaster. Amanda Bybee, founder of Amicus Solar O&M Cooperative, noted in a 2020 interview[151] that over the years she's come to a realization about what really matters, and her words ring true:

What I've really taken away are the people and the relationships, and finally the realization that success is not defined by business metrics. There are all of these clichés like you don't live to work, you work to live, that takes on more meaning as you get older; [you] cease to define yourself by revenue or profit.

As I look back at even my formative experiences with the Solar Austin campaign, fresh out of college, it's the friendships that grew out of that, that I've taken with me. Yes, I'm proud of the work we did, and yes that work is critical. But that's not what I take away with me, and it's such a shift in the way that you define success.

It goes along with the concept of measuring what matters, not just looking at traditional metrics KPI's. It's not 'I am successful today because I made a sale' or 'because I onboarded a new

---

[151] https://www.mysuncast.com/suncast-episodes/240

member company.' *I am successful today because I helped improve someone's life or I got to have an amazing heart to heart with my kid. It's revolutionary. It changes the whole definition of what you're chasing in life.*

We can all fall victim to the relentless pursuit of success, and society's veneration of it. But vanity for vanity's sake is empty. There are many books written on this subject but it's worth a reminder. Take time every day to enjoy your friends and family. Find gratification in the things that inspire you, whatever they might be, and no matter how trivial they may seem. That is your truth, and in the end, those are the things that truly matter.

Giving Back

At some point, after establishing yourself it's critical to pay forward the support that got you to where you are. For many that means mentorship, charity, or volunteering. Whatever it means to you make sure it's a focal point and that you create the space in your life.

Giving back requires time, resources, or both. Figure out what balance makes the most sense in your life and schedule it. Whether it's recurring donations or volunteering once a month, the benefits of these activities can stretch well beyond positive karma. Noble actions like these can lead to other less altruistic benefits too like growing your network, gaining new skills, padding your resumé, lowering stress, and creating new opportunities.

Leaders in cleantech have a lot to offer others in the community. Many non-profits are looking for board members to share their expertise. Find open board positions easily online at one of many job boards like bridgespan.org.

Many prospective career-seekers are looking for advice; let them take you out to lunch or buy you coffee – a pretty low barrier for someone to gain valuable insight. Or invest in someone's future through Big Brothers & Big Sisters. Make a point to help those who could really benefit, regardless of whether they can take you to happy hour at Applebee's.[152]

Whichever approach is ultimately best suited to you, be deliberate about how you're engaging.

A Green & Equitable Future with GRID Alternatives

According to the EPA, Environmental Justice is defined as "the fair treatment and meaningful involvement of all people regardless of race, color, national origin, or income, with respect to the development, implementation, and enforcement of environmental laws, regulations, and policies." From the EPA website:[153]

The environmental justice movement was started by individuals, primarily people of color, who sought to address the inequity of environmental protection in their communities.

Professor Robert Bullard wrote, 'whether, by conscious design or institutional neglect, communities of color in urban ghettos, in rural 'poverty pockets', or on economically impoverished Native-American reservations face some of the worst environmental devastation in the nation.'

The Civil Rights Movement of the 1960s sounded the alarm about the public health dangers for their families, their communities, and themselves.

---

[152] Please don't go to Applebee's for happy hour, or any hour.
[153] https://www.epa.gov/environmentaljustice

It is precisely because of these injustices that the clean energy transition must engage disadvantaged communities because they have been the hardest hit from generations of environmental malice.

Enter purpose-driven organizations like GRID Alternatives whose mission is "to make renewable energy technology and job training accessible to underserved communities." According to their website, "GRID is a leading voice in low-income solar policy and the nation's largest nonprofit solar installer, serving families throughout California, Colorado, the Mid-Atlantic region, and tribal communities nationwide. Our Energy For All Program (formerly Solar Affordable Housing Program) offers single-family, multifamily and community solar installation services, project development, and technical assistance, and we offer multiple levels of workforce development and service-learning opportunities, from volunteerism to in-depth solar training and paid internships. In addition, GRID's international program partners with communities in Nicaragua, Nepal, and Mexico to address their energy access issues."

And their numbers are impressive. As of early 2020, the organization had installed 13,316 systems, equaling 58.2 megawatts, providing $388,896,262 in lifetime savings, preventing over 1 million tons of GHG emissions, and training 44,732 participants since its 2001 inception. For obvious reasons, they've become one of the leading voices on equity in clean energy.

In a 2020 interview[154] policy and regulatory manager, Alexandra Wyatt remarked that "the biggest challenge [to their work] is combining the need for speed and scale with the need to make sure environmental justice communities and leaders can have their voices heard. Within these communities, we have to

---

[154] https://www.mysuncast.com/suncast-episodes/242

move things at the speed of trust, but you also have to move things very fast to meet the challenges of the current climate timeline. That's what gives me anxiety, will we hit the equity and the climate fast enough and well enough? We [have to] include everyone's voices, perspectives, expertise, and creativity."

Wyatt explained GRID's efforts, in particular, have been "a real win-win, and the industry has been really receptive to these training programs. We work closely with employment partners who are thrilled to have a more diverse workforce that looks more like the communities they serve but with a baseline experience that can help them hit the ground running."

Co-founder and CEO Erika Mackie outlined the diversity issue facing many solar (and cleantech) companies more broadly in a 2019 Greentech Media article[155]:

The results from The Solar Foundation and the Solar Energy Industries Association's second U.S. Solar Industry Diversity Study, released this spring, are clear: We've all got a lot more work to do.

Eighty-eight percent of senior executives in the solar industry are white and 80 percent are men. Demographic studies are important because they speak to deeper underlying inequities within the solar industry and society as a whole. The Solar Foundation study found women represented only 26 percent of the solar industry workforce and that men are more likely to earn higher wages than women in all positions — 26 percent more than women on average.

Rightly, the Solar Foundation also focuses on the unique experiences of women of color in the industry. Forty-two percent of black women reported feeling they had to "provide more evidence of their competence than their peers in other genders or races" (compared to 29 percent of white women and 16 percent of men).

---

[155] https://www.greentechmedia.com/articles/read/advancing-social-equity-in-solar-requires-data-and-honest-conversations

Conscious and unconscious biases harm people of color, and especially women of color, in our industry and make it difficult for talented people to get their foot in the door and to advance to senior ranks.

The key message here is to keep the door open for those behind you. Beyond that, it's important to make sure that you're actively giving others a hand up.

A Hand Up

It's nearly impossible for anyone to be a truly "self-made" person. Everybody's benefited from mentors, lucky breaks, teachers, and critical help that manifests itself in a myriad of ways. Aside from college scholarships and a great primary education, I owe a lot to my family.

Taking a step back (way back), I learned a lot about life from my grandparents Wayne and Cathy. As a single mother in her early twenties, my mom worked a lot. The toll of being a single parent and only child was hard; we were lucky to have my grandparents so close in our lives.

I had a modest upbringing in East St. Paul, but my family did an amazing job of making it seem like we had the world. Wayne did a lot: throwing baseballs after dinner, driving me before dawn on weekends to carry golf clubs for rich people, and, among many other things, taught me the value of honesty and perseverance.

Post-college and early on at IPS Wayne was a great sounding board. Both he and my grandmother were sincerely interested in what I did. Never a salesperson himself, Wayne has a real gift for connecting with others in a way I can only struggle to emulate. The type of guy to effortlessly strike up a conversation with anyone, he's both genuine and relatable.

Wayne with my daughter Cate in 2017 at Eichten Hidden Acres

In 2010, Wayne introduced me to a man named Ed Eichten. For decades, Wayne worked as a chemist at 3M, and Ed worked there in security. Over the years they became friends, and when my grandfather retired and Ed moved back to his family cheese and buffalo farm in rural Minnesota they kept in touch.

On a particularly hot August day, Ed agreed to my proposal to install solar panels for their cheese factory. He's a lot like Wayne, in that he'd be the most down-to-earth, charismatic guy in the room regardless of where you were or who you were with. Not wanting to let either of them down, I had all the motivation needed to ensure the project went smoothly.

One of the many interviews with Ed Eichten regarding his community solar project

I worked hard to deliver on my promises, and by the same time a year later the panels were up and operating. That process was a crash-course in development: I pulled together interconnection agreements, filed grant paperwork, and helped his banker to underwrite the $200,000 loan. Ed is still the best client I've ever had.

Our early success led to a very easy conversation two years later in 2013 when I outlined a concept of leasing his entire 40-acre hay field for a Community Solar Garden. I had no idea what I was doing at the time. But much of those early days in my career was about faking it until I made it.

We formally announced Chisago County's first Community Solar project in June 2014. It wasn't necessarily going to be the first, nor was it necessarily going to happen – but that didn't stop us from being bold. The development process included utility applications, local permitting, financing, and a lot more – all of which required the help of many people – it was similar to what we'd done a few years earlier, but at a much greater scale (125x to be exact).

At a launch event that August, we set up a tent with some embarrassingly amateur visual renderings and cheese plates. Surprisingly, a lot of people showed up – politicians, potential partners and competitors, residents – it was pretty wild. I tiptoed around a thousand questions that mainly centered around whether or not the project would actually happen. "Hell yes...?" was my somewhat tepid response.

That fall applications were made and financing fell in place. It was very strange how everything lined up for the project to become viable, almost like we had willed it into existence. Nearly two years to the day from when we announced, construction began and we were off to the races.

Selfie at the Red Wing Solar Garden

Those first few projects spawned a handful more, then a dozen. There were slam dunks, and excruciating negotiations where I was sure everything would spiral into disaster. Some enemies turned into allies and some colleagues into good friends. I started to see our solar installations from airplanes, and at some point, regretfully, I couldn't physically visit each site in person anymore – first world problems.

Young America Solar Garden, by plane

Remember that first 2-panel hot water project? The Eichten's Community Solar Garden has about 20,000 PV panels, providing subscribers with more than $100,000 in annual net savings, and offsets nearly 2,000,000 pounds of CO_2 per year. As of 2020 our Community Solar projects in aggregate are producing about 40 times as much impact; it's been an insane and immensely rewarding ride. But I recognize that nothing is done in a vacuum, and I'll be forever thankful to those who have given me a hand up.

The last four years have been the craziest and most rewarding of my life, not the least of which because I've gotten to see Cate grow into a beautiful 5-year old firecracker who will no doubt light up the world soon, and I've gotten to know Lil' Lili, 18 months and every bit her sister's equal. Firmly in my mid-30's, life has accelerated so quickly, as it will for most of you, if it hasn't already. My wish is that you'll all be as fortunate as I have been, because the world needs us to succeed.

There are many obstacles standing between us and a better future, but there is hope. If clean energy is now your path – cheers to your commitment! I expect we'll toast many milestones together on our way to defeating the climate crisis and changing the world.

Afterword

The genesis of this book was a mix of hubris and third-life crisis during 2019 and 2020. A lot was happening at the time; business was booming, our second daughter was just born, the emergence of Covid19 shut the planet down, and the murder of George Floyd thrust our community into a moment of reckoning. One upshot of isolation was that it provided just enough focus to finalize this manuscript.

Reflection can be both good and bad, which made these chapters very bittersweet. After more than a dozen years in renewable energy, it truly feels like I'm coming to the end of one era and beginning the next. I've been extremely lucky. I'm happy to share this information with a touch of grief, humility, and gratitude.

I'm very thankful for the help that I've received along the way. One way to give back is to pay forward the opportunity and knowledge to others. Your success in clean energy could mean the difference between keeping temperatures increases below 1.5 degrees Celsius. The fact that this industry is so new and the ladder to the top is so much shorter gives me a ton of hope for our future.

On a slightly more cynical note there is some shaming that needs to happen too. Many think the coddling of millennials is responsible for today's worldwide death spiral. We've destroyed the rainforests and Blockbuster Video. After continuously hitting snooze on adulthood, we're waking up. Mom won't do our laundry anymore and we can't get extra credit in the real world, so our lives are shattered.

As an older and wiser millennial, I think it's funny we get blamed for everyone's problems. The truth is that previous generations have fleeced our future: we're trillions in debt, forced into servitude for health care and education, all while inheriting a planet that's past the boiling point. It's no wonder we crawled back to our parents' basements with an extra-large bottle of Xanax. The "fragile" state we're in is a direct result of previous generations' recklessness.

By most statistical measures we're working harder, achieving more, but earning less; it's hard to appreciate anything "given" to us. Gen-Y and Z will probably solve this shitty rubix cube, but only when we log off Fortnite and TikTok long enough to focus on this crisis with the level of immediacy it demands. A crisis not of our own creation, but which now is our burden, and opportunity.

Contrary to my emo-esque rant I am truly optimistic. I'm optimistic for the exact same reasons laid out in this book. In the face of seemingly insurmountable odds, the exponential adoption of clean energy technology will transform the future in much the same way that automobiles changed transportation and personal computers revolutionized the information age. We'll win not because "it's the right thing to do," but because it's the least expensive and most reliable option. A distributed energy future means more resiliency and security, more economic development in rural America, more high-paying jobs that can't be outsourced - oh and a cleaner grid.

The electrification of the transportation and heating sectors is providing more flexible loads, and large batteries are making clean energy production dispatchable. Smart grids orchestrate the balance between producers and consumers in real time by the nanosecond. Microgrids are allowing entire communities to sustainably isolate themselves and, in some areas of the world, skip traditional and costly centralized power systems deployed by 20th century industrial economies.

All of this is happening at lightning speed. One of my favorite stats is that 98.2% of all global solar photovoltaic capacity *ever* has been installed in the decade directly preceding 2019.[156] From 2000 to 2018 US wind and solar capacity increased 4,000% and 55,000% respectively. According to NREL data it took more than 40 years for the domestic solar market to reach 1% penetration in 2015, and less than 3 years to double it. Wind and battery storage have parallel stories, and electric vehicle adoption is on a similar path.

Career opportunities are also promising. There are now more jobs in Clean Energy than the oil and coal industry combined.[157] 3.3 million Americans working in clean energy, and we're expanding on an exponential curve.

This is a generational opportunity to reduce inequalities and the wealth gap. On average under-resourced households pay 2.5 times more for energy as a percentage of their income compared to their wealthier counterparts. Modest green improvements could reduce their energy burden by an average of $1,500 annually. From a public health standpoint, reducing emissions could prevent nearly 300,000 premature US deaths caused by air pollution *each year*.

Green power has the opportunity to bridge divides. 7 in 10 Americans think clean energy should be a high or very high

---

[156] https://en.wikipedia.org/wiki/Growth_of_photovoltaics#Worldwide_annual_deployment
[157] US Department of Energy 2017 U.S. Energy and Employment Report

priority for the president and congress. Clean power helps rural communities by providing diversified income for farmers and new tax revenue for local governments.

We are all standing on the shoulders of giants, my Ohana. In order to honor everything that came before us and all that's yet to come, we should align with our passions, make some money, and save the planet. The time is now.

Acknowledgments

To my Ohana, without you none of this would have been possible. My grandparents Wayne and Cathy, my mom Kristine, my dad George – thank you for all of your love and sacrifices. Dana, Lilian, and Cate – you keep me going when things get hard. My sister and brothers, Meleane and Benj(nephew TBD), Junior, and George. In memory of all those who came before including uncle T, uncle Sione, my braddah in heaven Nase. To all the cousins, aunties, and uncles – Ofa. Uncle Greg & Sharon, Mike & Ali, Andrew & Shane, Shelly – much love.

To my ride or dies: Will, Amy, Jodie, Ron, Nancy, Tambo, Jake, Casey, Nikki, Linda, Nate, Nicci, Lars, Phil, Sarah, Kelly, Chris, Mark, Vanesa, Jena, Micah, Jer, Benny, Luca., Archer, Hill – Anything is Pasible! To my musical family: Mark (again), Vuthy, Connor, Chris, Paul, Rob, Cory, Adam, Dan, Justin, Kyle, Bob, Adam, Nate, Jeff – play on players.

To my IPS family, especially Ralph, Jamie, Kyle, Andy, Hanson, Kim – your efforts have continued to inspire me beyond words. Evan-I'll forever ride your coattails as long as you let me. Clean energy friends including Matt, Sanjiv, Gautam, Jake, Dean, David S., Gregg M., Michael N., Liz L., Doug S., Julian B., Geoff, Norm, Justin, Pablo, Morgan, Buzz – mahalo.

To my incredible clients including Ed, Pat D., Alan S., Dan S., Mike & Lisa C, Lisa J., Mark F., and so many others – your trust has meant so much!

To those who helped with this book including Megan, Matt D., Thomas H. – your efforts are appreciated, even if perfectionism will never let me believe this is complete.

To all the educators in my life that inspired me along the way – thank you. To the coaches, community members, and others who invested their time and energy I'll forever be thankful.

Last but not least, thank *you*. Good luck on your journey wherever it might take you and may we all have a little luck in tackling the challenges ahead.

Cheers,

Eric Pasi

Resources

American Council on Renewable Energy (ACORE) – nonprofit organization accelerating the renewable energy transition, with content and resources: https://acore.org/

Cleantech Open – annual startup contest that fosters green entrepreneurs and their ideas: https://www.cleantechopen.org/

Climate Reality Project – climate solutions advocacy and training hub: https://www.climaterealityproject.org/

ClimateBase – green career job board: https://climatebase.org

Creating Climate Wealth (book) –by author and entrepreneur Jigar Shah, outlining the pathway to unlocking the impact economy: https://www.amazon.com/Creating-Climate-Wealth-Unlocking-Economy/dp/0989353109

Database of State Incentives for Renewables & Efficiency (DSIRE) – comprehensive source for US state and federal policies affecting the clean energy development: https://www.dsireusa.org/

Energy News Network – national news outlet covering energy issues, primarily focused on US renewables markets: https://energynews.us/

Energy Storage Association – industry association with online resources for advocates of this emerging technology: https://energystorage.org/

Environmental & Energy Study Institute – non-profit advocacy organization dedicated to promoting the transition to a low-emissions economy: https://www.eesi.org/

Green America – social and environmental activism publication with plenty of content including divestment and sustainable food practices: https://www.greenamerica.org/

Green Jobs Network – the largest global clean energy job board http://www.greenjobs.net/

Green For All – subgroup of Dream Corps focused on the intersection of the environmental, economic, and racial justice movements: https://www.thedreamcorps.org/our-programs/green-for-all/

Greentech Media – online media outlet dedicated to covering clean energy issues: https://www.greentechmedia.com/

GRID Alternatives – nation's largest non-profit solar installer focusing on access for under-resourced communities, providing training and volunteer opportunities: https://gridalternatives.org/

National Renewable Energy Laboratories – research institution on the forefront of clean energy innovation, with online tools like PVWatts: https://www.nrel.gov/

North American Windpower – publication covering on and off-shore wind developments: https://nawindpower.com/

Office of Energy Efficiency & Renewable Energy – clean energy jobs and planning hub with various tools and resources: https://www.energy.gov/eere/education/clean-energy-jobs-and-planning

Project Drawdown – advocacy non-profit aimed at moving climate solutions forward: https://drawdown.org/

Solar Power World – US solar focused print and e-publication: https://www.solarpowerworldonline.com/

Solar Wakeup – influential solar newsletter, blog and podcast: https://www.solarwakeup.com/

Suncast Media – popular solar energy podcast with insights for developing a clean energy career: https://mysuncast.com/

US Green Building Council – certifying organization for commercial (and residential) sustainable buildings: https://www.usgbc.org/

Utility Dive – in-depth journalism on utility industry trends: https://www.utilitydive.com/

Notes

Notes

About the Author

Eric Pasi is a clean energy entrepreneur and climate warrior who's helped shape the US renewable energy landscape since 2007. He's led in various capacities including principal and Chief Development Officer of Impact Power Solutions (formerly IPS Solar), the top Midwest commercial solar development company according to Solar Power World Magazine. There he's helped to increase revenues by over 2,000%, becoming one of the fastest-growing companies in the country according to Inc Magazine.

In recent years he's been dedicated to solar & schools initiatives, clean energy access issues, and Community Solar. In total Eric has helped contribute to over 200 megawatts of solar development in the upper Midwest, enough energy for nearly 30,000 average homes.

Aside from business he's continued to be a vocal advocate and grassroots activist for environmental groups. He's served industry groups like the North American Board of Certified Energy Practitioners and as a board member for the Minnesota Solar Energy Industries Association and regional policy powerhouse Fresh Energy.

He's passionate about solving the climate crisis, and paying forward the same opportunities afforded to him, to the next generation of clean energy leaders.

linkedin.com/in/ericpasi (LinkedIn)
@ericpasi (twitter) @anythingispasible (instagram)

Made in the USA
Monee, IL
27 January 2021